Learning Windows 8 Game Development

Learn how to develop exciting tablet and PC games for Windows 8 using practical, hands-on examples

Michael Quandt

PUBLISHING

BIRMINGHAM - MUMBAI

Learning Windows 8 Game Development

First published: October 2013

Production Reference: 1181013

Published by Packt Publishing Ltd.
Livery Place
35 Livery Street
Birmingham B3 2PB, UK.

ISBN 978-1-84969-744-6

www.packtpub.com

Cover Image by Suresh Mogre (suresh.mogre.99@gmail.com)

Credits

Author
Michael Quandt

Reviewers
Anthony E. Alvarez
Laurent Couvidou
Hexuan
Andrei Marukovich
Mark Sinnathamby

Acquisition Editor
Antony Lowe

Lead Technical Editor
Chalini Snega Victor

Technical Editors
Vrinda Nitesh Bhosale
Ritika Singh

Project Coordinator
Kranti Berde

Proofreaders
Lawrence A. Herman
Christopher Smith

Indexer
Monica Ajmera Mehta

Graphics
Ronak Dhruv
Yuvraj Mannari

Production Coordinator
Prachali Bhiwandkar

Cover Work
Prachali Bhiwandkar

About the Author

Michael Quandt has been working with games, from XNA to DirectX to Unity, as a hobbyist and professional for four years. He has spoken at local game development conferences and workshops while working with Microsoft Australia as a Technical Evangelist. Since then he has contributed to the translation of multiple major franchise games to the Windows Store platform, and continues to work with local developers and students to get them involved in game development and bringing their best to the Windows platform.

About the Reviewers

Anthony E. Alvarez is a native New Yorker. His hobbies include photography, singing, and cooking. He is a food activist and a political atheist. He loves the great outdoors and travelling.

Anthony has held positions such as Software Engineer, Webmaster, Unix Administrator, Customer Service Representative, Marketing Systems Manager, and Salesforce.com Database Administrator. He speaks three foreign languages: Chinese, Japanese, and Spanish.

After returning from a study abroad scholarship in Guangzhou, China, Anthony changed his major to Asian Studies. While attending university, he worked at IBM for three semesters where he developed presentation materials for field sales teams. After graduating CCNY with a Bachelors degree in Arts (BA), Anthony was hired as a computer consultant by a Japanese Architecture company. His clients included Tokyo Electric Power Company (TEPCO), IBM Japan, Taisei Construction, Nippon Telephone and Telegraph (NTT), Budweiser Japan, and Polaroid Japan.

After working three years in Tokyo, Anthony returned to the USA and settled in the Boston Metro area. He was employee number 3 of a startup company specializing in e-commerce projects. Anthony taught adult education courses on e-commerce.

Four years later, Anthony moved to Atlanta to become the first webmaster at Panasonic Wireless Research and Design Center (PMCDU). The company was designing a flagship smart phone for the American market.

Moving to New Jersey, he held the position of a web marketing manager at Casio America, Inc.

Currently a director at Pucho Web Solutions, Anthony specializes in marketing and e-commerce projects using Open Source Software. In order to manage business development issues at the firm, Anthony has completed Entrepreneurship training from Workshop in Business Opportunities (WIBO.org) and Kauffman FastTrac (Kauffman.org). Anthony is a Free Culture advocate using open source methods and tools. He is a volunteer copy editor for the Wikipedia project, an online encyclopedia.

One of his specialties at Pucho Web Solutions is video. He is a producer of both web and broadcast TV video. His programs have been broadcasted on stations in Manhattan, Brooklyn, Staten Island, and Queens Cable TV.

In the performing arts, Anthony has appeared on TV shows that are shot on location in New York City including White Collar, Law & Order, Nurse Jackie, Gossip Girl, Blue Bloods, and Girls.

For films, Anthony has played a role as a diplomat in Junji Sakamoto's upcoming financial thriller Human Trust (Jinrui Shikin), which is scheduled to debut in Japan on October 19, 2013. Human Trust, directed by Junji Sakamoto, is a story of an international financial conspiracy seeking to right the unfairness of the world, shot on location at United Nations (UN) General Assembly hall.

Follow Anthony at his blog: `http://www.AnthonyAlvarez.us`.

Pucho Web Solutions (`http://www.PuchoWebsolutions.com`) provides web marketing solutions to small businesses in Manhattan by showcasing multimedia-based content on your website using video, web photo albums, and audio. Pucho Web Solutions marketing services help you tell your story, engage your audience, and increase web traffic at your site.

Laurent Couvidou is a professional game developer with experiences at 10tacle Studios, Ubisoft Montpellier, and TriOviz, among others. Besides these daily jobs, he also participated in several amateur game jams.

Hexuan fell in love with video game programming in high school. After graduation, he worked in listed companies working on Android, iOS game development. He participated in cocos2dx for a Win8 open source project and has many years of game programming experience.

Hexuan loves technology, is curious about new technologies, and believes that technology makes human life better.

Thanks to my family. I love you.

Andrei Marukovich is a technical lead at AB SCIEX and Microsoft C# MVP. Andrei has been developing software professionally for over 15 years. During this time he has designed and developed applications in such diverse areas as life science, semiconductor device manufacturing, robotics, and game development. Andrei can be found online at `http://lunarfrog.com`. He lives in Toronto with his beautiful wife and daughter.

Mark Sinnathamby is a software engineer and .NET consultant, living and working in Singapore. He has developed many diverse types of software-intensive systems, and worked in a variety of technological domains. In his spare time, he loves to study game design and development, initially starting with OpenGL, and now experimenting and working with Microsoft DirectX technology.

www.PacktPub.com

Support files, eBooks, discount offers and more

You might want to visit www.PacktPub.com for support files and downloads related to your book.

Did you know that Packt offers eBook versions of every book published, with PDF and ePub files available? You can upgrade to the eBook version at www.PacktPub.com and as a print book customer, you are entitled to a discount on the eBook copy. Get in touch with us at service@packtpub.com for more details.

At www.PacktPub.com, you can also read a collection of free technical articles, sign up for a range of free newsletters and receive exclusive discounts and offers on Packt books and eBooks.

http://PacktLib.PacktPub.com

Do you need instant solutions to your IT questions? PacktLib is Packt's online digital book library. Here, you can access, read and search across Packt's entire library of books.

Why Subscribe?

- Fully searchable across every book published by Packt
- Copy and paste, print and bookmark content
- On demand and accessible via web browser

Free Access for Packt account holders

If you have an account with Packt at www.PacktPub.com, you can use this to access PacktLib today and view nine entirely free books. Simply use your login credentials for immediate access.

Table of Contents

Preface

With the rising popularity of mobile platforms such as phones and tablets, the games industry has found a new market eager for more and more games. With the introduction of Windows 8, Microsoft has entered this market, bringing years of experience and widely-used game development technologies such as Direct3D. In this book, we will take a look at how you can get started making a game for Windows 8, so you can sell to both the desktop and tablet markets. Through this book you'll learn how to develop a simple side-scrolling space shooter, and enhance the game with Windows 8 features such as Share Charm integration and Live Tiles.

What this book covers

Chapter 1, Getting Started with Direct3D, looks at how we can initialize Direct3D in Windows 8 and prepare all of the resources to display something on the screen.

Chapter 2, Drawing 2D Sprites, is where we will take our first steps into drawing images on the screen. You'll learn about the different concepts involved in drawing 2D images, as well as some useful libraries to make 2D rendering even easier.

Chapter 3, Adding the Input, will teach you how to read from the touch screen, keyboard, mouse, and GamePad to implement the interactive element of your game.

Chapter 4, Adding the Play in the Gameplay, will show you how to structure your game and add the mechanics that make the game fun. We'll look at code structure and the subsystems you will need to complete the game.

Chapter 5, Tilting the World, is an introduction to the sensors on the device that will enable new gameplay genres and opportunities. You will learn about the different options available and how to easily work with them to get different types of input.

Chapter 6, Bragging Rights, will look at the Share Charm and Live Tiles in Windows 8. Here you will learn how to take advantage of these features to quickly add support for social media, and keep your players engaged outside of the game.

Chapter 7, Playing Games with Friends, looks at the networking options available in Windows 8, as well as how to add a user interface system to support this.

Chapter 8, Getting into the Store, will lift the lid on the Windows Store submission and certification process. We'll look at the important things to remember, as well as some tips and tricks to make certification painless.

Chapter 9, Monetization, investigates the different options and methods you can use to make some money from your game.

Appendix, Adding the Third Dimension, will give a light introduction to the next step in game development: 3D. You will learn the basic concepts involved so you know where to start when you want to add in another dimension to your game.

What you need for this book

You only need two pieces of software to get started with this book:

- Windows 8
- Visual Studio 2012 (or higher)

Visual Studio 2012 is Microsoft's development environment, and is used for all forms of Windows development, from desktop to store. There are a few editions of Visual Studio with different prices; however, a free version, named Visual Studio 2012 Express Edition, can be downloaded from:

```
http://www.microsoft.com/visualstudio/eng/downloads#express-win8
```

If you have access to higher editions of Visual Studio 2012, you can use those as well, and most functions should be in the same place.

 This book has been written for Visual Studio 2012 and is correct at the time of writing. Future versions of Visual Studio as well as Windows 8 may be different.

NuGet and DirectXTK

NuGet is a development package manager. If you've used package managers in POSIX environments, you'll recognise the concept, only here it's for third-party libraries. NuGet officially supports C# and C++, and will quickly become an essential tool in your Windows development toolbox.

NuGet is integrated into all versions of Visual Studio from 2012 onwards, and adding a "package" to your project is as easy as right-clicking on your project in the **Solution Explorer** and selecting **Manage NuGet Packages**. From there you can search for packages and easily install them to your project with a single click. Any dependencies will be automatically installed, and if required your project will be configured to support the new library.

MSDN

The final resource that you might want to have access to is MSDN (www.msdn.com). MSDN (Microsoft Developer Network) is the one-stop shop for documentation on all Microsoft technology. This book will contain links to MSDN pages with documentation with for further reading. If you have any questions or need to know the details on an API, make this your first stop.

Languages and other resources

Although most of the book will be developed using standard C++11, some parts will require the use of the new C++ Component Extensions (C++/CX) from Microsoft. Alongside that we will avoid going into detail about the new WinRT platform outside of the APIs you need to develop your game, so if you want to learn more about these technologies, read through the quick summary that follows, and take a look at the provided reference links for further reading.

WinRT

WinRT is the new API layer used by Windows Store applications to replace Win32. This new API provides a cleaner and easier way to work with the operating system, and also enables cross-language library development using WinRT Components.

 When developing a Windows Store application, you do not need to include any headers; they are all automatically included during compile tile to save you the trouble.

For a detailed look at the WinRT type system and how it works, visit:

```
http://blogs.microsoft.co.il/blogs/sasha/archive/2011/09/17/under-
the-covers-of-winrt-using-c.aspx
```

Components

WinRT Components allow you to share code between the three Windows Store languages: C++, C#, and JavaScript. All public code in a component must use the `ref class` from C++/CX. This is because the component needs to ensure it can communicate with the other languages, which do not support pointers and other C++ specific concepts. If you want to use plain C++ within the component, you need to specify the visibility as `internal`.

We will look at creating a WinRT component later in the book. However, for more information, visit:

```
http://msdn.microsoft.com/en-us/library/windows/apps/hh441569
```

Threading

WinRT uses a new threading model based on the concept of asynchronous development using futures and continuations. This means that instead of creating background code in a traditional manner, you can specify code to run asynchronously, and then append the code that "continues" after the original code finishes. This is done using Tasks, which represent code that runs asynchronously, and at some point in the future may return an object (or value).

For more information on the threading and async model used in WinRT, visit:

```
http://msdn.microsoft.com/en-us/magazine/hh781020.aspx
```

C++ Component Extensions

C++ Component Extensions are a set of keywords that Microsoft has added to C++ to make it easier to work with WinRT and COM. These extensions simply enhance the language. They are required for the WinRT APIs, but can be avoided everywhere else if desired.

For more information on C++/CX, including a language reference, visit:

```
http://msdn.microsoft.com/en-us/library/windows/apps/hh699871
```

Who this book is for

This book is intended for developers who already have a good grasp of C++ development. You should know the basic programming concepts such as object-oriented programming. Knowledge of older Windows technologies such as **Component Object Model (COM)** will be useful but is not required.

Conventions

In this book, you will find a number of styles of text that distinguish between different kinds of information. Here are some examples of these styles, and an explanation of their meaning.

Code words in text, database table names, folder names, filenames, file extensions, pathnames, dummy URLs, user input, and Twitter handles are shown as follows: "To compile this you'll also need to ensure that any `#include` statements that previously pointed to `CubeRenderer.h` now point to `Game.h`."

A block of code is set as follows:

```
#pragma once
#include "Direct3DBase.h"
ref class Game sealed : public Direct3DBase
{
  public:
    Game();
    virtual void Render() override;
    void Update(float totalTime, float deltaTime);
};
```

New terms and **important words** are shown in bold. Words that you see on the screen, in menus or dialog boxes for example, appear in the text like this: " You can find this project in the same window by navigating to **New Project | Templates | Visual C++ | Windows Store**".

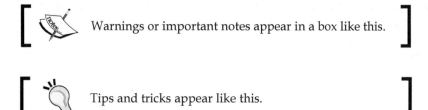

[Warnings or important notes appear in a box like this.]

[Tips and tricks appear like this.]

Reader feedback

Feedback from our readers is always welcome. Let us know what you think about this book—what you liked or may have disliked. Reader feedback is important for us to develop titles that you really get the most out of.

To send us general feedback, simply send an e-mail to feedback@packtpub.com, and mention the book title via the subject of your message.

If there is a topic that you have expertise in and you are interested in either writing or contributing to a book, see our author guide on www.packtpub.com/authors.

Customer support

Now that you are the proud owner of a Packt Publishing book, we have a number of things to help you to get the most from your purchase.

Downloading the example code

You can download the example code files for all Packt Publishing books you have purchased from your account at http://www.packtpub.com. If you purchased this book elsewhere, you can visit http://www.packtpub.com/support and register to have the files e-mailed directly to you.

Errata

Although we have taken every care to ensure the accuracy of our content, mistakes do happen. If you find a mistake in one of our books—maybe a mistake in the text or the code—we would be grateful if you would report this to us. By doing so, you can save other readers from frustration and help us improve subsequent versions of this book. If you find any errata, please report them by visiting http://www.packtpub.com/submit-errata, selecting your book, clicking on the **errata submission form** link, and entering the details of your errata. Once your errata are verified, your submission will be accepted and the errata will be uploaded on our website, or added to any list of existing errata, under the Errata section of that title. Any existing errata can be viewed by selecting your title from http://www.packtpub.com/support.

Piracy

Piracy of copyright material on the Internet is an ongoing problem across all media. At Packt Publishing, we take the protection of our copyright and licenses very seriously. If you come across any illegal copies of our works, in any form, on the Internet, please provide us with the location address or website name immediately so that we can pursue a remedy.

Please contact us at copyright@packtpub.com with a link to the suspected pirated material.

We appreciate your help in protecting our authors, and our ability to bring you valuable content.

Questions

You can contact us at questions@packtpub.com if you are having a problem with any aspect of the book, and we will do our best to address it.

1
Getting Started with Direct3D

They say the first steps are the hardest, and beginning a new game is no exception. Therefore, we should use as much help as possible to make those first steps easier, and get into the fun parts of game development. To support the new WinRT platform, we need some new templates, and there are plenty to be had in Visual Studio 2012. Most important to us is the Direct3D App template, which provides the base code for a C++ Windows Store application, without any of the XAML that the other templates include.

The template that we've chosen will provide us with the code to create a WinRT window, as well as the code for the Direct3D components that will allow us to create the game world. This chapter will focus on explaining the code included so that you understand how it all works, as well as the changes needed to prepare the project for our own code.

In this chapter we will cover the following topics:

- Creating the application window
- Initialising Direct3D
- Direct3D devices and contexts
- Render targets and depth buffers
- The graphics pipeline
- What a game loop looks like
- Clearing and presenting the screen

Setting up the stage

Let's begin by starting up Visual Studio 2012 (the Express Edition is fine) and creating a new Direct3D App project. You can find this project in the same window by navigating to **New Project | Templates | Visual C++ | Windows Store**. Once Visual Studio has finished creating the project, we need to delete the following files:

- `CubeRenderer.h`
- `CubeRenderer.cpp`
- `SimpleVertexShader.hlsl`
- `SimplePixelShader.hlsl`

Once these files have been removed, we need to remove any references to the files that we just removed. Now create a new header (`Game.h`) and code (`Game.cpp`) file and add the following class declaration and some stub functions into `Game.h` and `Game.cpp`, respectively. Once you've done that, search for any references to `CubeRenderer` and replace them with `Game`. To compile this you'll also need to ensure that any `#include` statements that previously pointed to `CubeRenderer.h` now point to `Game.h`.

 Remember that Microsoft introduced the C++/CX (Component Extensions) to help you write C++ code that works with WinRT. Make sure that you're creating the right type of class.

```
#pragma once
#include "Direct3DBase.h"
ref class Game sealed : public Direct3DBase
{
  public:
    Game();
    virtual void Render() override;
    void Update(float totalTime, float deltaTime);
};
```

 Downloading the example code

You can download the example code files for all Packt books you have purchased from your account at http://www.packtpub.com. If you purchased this book elsewhere, you can visit http://www.packtpub.com/support and register to have the files e-mailed directly to you.

Here we have the standard constructor, as well as an overridden `Render()` function from the `Direct3DBase` base class. Alongside, we have a new function named `Update()`, which will be explained in more detail when we cover the **game loop** later in this chapter.

We add the following stub methods in Game.cpp to allow this to compile:

```
#include "pch.h"
#include "Game.h"

Game::Game(void)
{
}

void Game::Render()
{
}

void Game::Update(float totalTime, float deltaTime)
{
}
```

Once these are in place you can compile to ensure everything works fine, before we move on to the rest of the basic game structure.

Applications and windows

Windows 8 applications use a different window system compared to the Win32 days. When the application starts, instead of describing a window that needs to be created, you provide an implementation of **IFrameworkView** that allows your application to respond to events such as resume, suspend, and resize.

When you implement this interface, you also have control over the system used to render to the screen, just as if you had created a Win32 window. In this book we will only use DirectX to create the visuals for the screen; however, Microsoft provides another option that can be used in conjunction with DirectX (or on its own). XAML is the user interface system that provides everything from controls to media to animations. If you want to avoid creating a user interface yourself, this would be your choice. However, because XAML uses DirectX for rendering, some extra steps need to be taken to ensure that the two work together properly. This is beyond the scope of the book, but I strongly recommend you look into taking those extra steps if you want to take advantage of an incredibly powerful user interface system.

The most important methods for us right now are `Initialize`, `SetWindow`, and `Run`, which can all be found in the `Chapter1` class (`Chapter1.h`) if you're following along with the sample code. These three methods are where we will hook up the code for the game. As of now, the template has already included some code referring to the `CubeRenderer`. To compile the code we need to replace any references to `CubeRenderer` inside our `Chapter1` class with a reference to `Game`.

Structuring each frame

All games start up, initialize, and run in a loop until it is time to close down and clean up. The big difference that games have over other applications is they will often load, reinitialize, and destroy content multiple times over the life of the process, as the player progresses through different levels or stages of the game.

Another difference lies in the interactive element of games. To create an immersive and responsive experience, games need to iterate through all of the subsystems, processing input and logic before presenting video and audio to the player at a high rate. Each video iteration presented to the player is called a **Frame**. The performance of games can be drawn from the number of frames that appear on the monitor in a second, which leads to the term **Frames Per Second** or **FPS** (not to be confused with First Person Shooter). Modern games need to process an incredible amount of data and repeatedly draw highly detailed objects 30-60 times per second, which means that they need to do all of the work in a short span of time. For modern games that claim to run at 60 FPS, this means that they need to complete all of the processing and rendering in under 1/60th of a second. Some games spread the processing across multiple frames, or make use of multithreading to allow intensive calculations, while still maintaining the desired frame rate. The key thing to ensure here is that the latency from user input to the result appearing on screen is minimized, as this can impact the player experience, depending on the type of game being developed.

The loop that operates at the frame rate of the game is called the game loop. In the days of Win32 games, there was a lot of discussion about the best way to structure the game loop so that the system would have enough time to process the operating system messages. Now that we have shifted from polling operating system messages to an event-based system, we no longer need to worry, and can instead just create a simple while loop to handle everything.

A modern game loop would look like the following:

```
while the game is running
{
  Update the timer
  Dispatch Events
  Update the Game State
  Draw the Frame
  Present the Frame to the Screen
}
```

Although we will later look at this loop in detail, there are two items that you might not expect. WinRT provides a method dispatch system that allows for the code to run on specific threads. This is important because now the operating system can generate events from different OS threads and we will only receive them on the main game thread (the one that runs the game loop). If you're using XAML, this becomes even more important as certain actions will crash if they are not run on the UI thread. By providing the dispatcher, we now have an easy way to fire off non-thread safe actions and ensure that they run on the thread we want them to.

The final item you may not have seen before involves presenting the frame to the screen. This will be covered in detail later in the chapter, but briefly, this is where we signal that we are done with drawing and the graphics API can take the final rendered frame and display it on the monitor.

Initializing the Direct3D API

Direct3D is a rendering API that allows you to write your game without having to worry about which graphics card or driver the user may have. By separating this concern through the **Component Object Model (COM)** system, you can easily write once and have your code run on the hardware from NVIDIA or AMD.

Now let's take a look at `Direct3DBase.cpp`, the class that we inherited from earlier. This is where DirectX is set up and prepared for use. There are a few objects that we need to create here to ensure we have everything required to start drawing.

Graphics device

The first is the graphics device, represented by an `ID3D11Device` object. The device represents the physical graphics card and the link to a single adapter. It is primarily used to create resources such as textures and shaders, and owns the device context and swap chain.

Direct3D 11.1 also supports the use of **feature levels** to support older graphics cards that may only support Direct3D 9.0 or Direct3D 10.0 features. When you create the device, you should specify a list of feature levels that your game will support, and DirectX will handle all of the checks to ensure you get the highest feature level you want that the graphics card supports.

You can find the code that creates the graphics device in the `Direct3DBase::CreateDeviceResources()` method. Here we allow all possible feature levels, which will allow our game to run on older and weaker devices. The key thing to remember here is that if you want to use any graphics features that were introduced after Direct3D 9.0, you will need to either remove the older feature levels from the list or manually check which level you have received and avoid using that feature.

Once we have a list of feature levels, we just need a simple call to the `D3D11CreateDevice()` method, which will provide us with the device and immediate device context.

 `nullptr` is a new C++11 keyword that gives us a strongly-defined null pointer. Previously NULL was just an alias for zero, which prevented the compiler from supporting us with extra error-checking.

```
D3D11CreateDevice(
    nullptr,
    D3D_DRIVER_TYPE_HARDWARE,
    nullptr,
    D3D11_CREATE_DEVICE_BGRA_SUPPORT,
    featureLevels,
    ARRAYSIZE(featureLevels),
    D3D11_SDK_VERSION,
    &device,
    &m_featureLevel,
    &context
    );
```

Most of this is pretty simple: we request a hardware device with BGRA format layout support (see the *Swap chain* section for more details on texture formats) and provide a list of feature levels that we can support. The magic of COM and Direct3D will provide us with an `ID3D11Device` and `ID3D11DeviceContext` that we can use for rendering.

Device context

The device context is probably the most useful item that you're going to create. This is where you will issue all draw calls and state changes to the graphics hardware. The device context works together with the graphics device to provide 99 percent of the commands you need to use Direct3D.

By default we get an **immediate context** along with our graphics device. One of the main benefits provided by a context system is the ability to issue commands from worker threads using **deferred contexts**. These deferred contexts can then be passed to the immediate context so that their commands can be issued on a single thread, allowing for multithreading with an API that is not thread-safe.

To create an immediate `ID3D11DeviceContext`, just pass a pointer to the same method that we used to create the device.

Deferred contexts are generally considered an advanced technique and are outside the scope of this book; however, if you're looking to take full advantage of modern hardware, you will want to take a look at this topic to ensure that you can work with the GPU without limiting yourself to a single CPU core.

If you're trying to remember which object to use when you're rendering, remember that the device is about creating resources throughout the lifetime of the application, while the device context does the work to apply those resources and create the images that are displayed to the user.

Swap chain

Working with Direct3D exposes you to a number of asynchronous devices, all operating at different rates independent of each other. If you drew to the same texture buffer that the monitor used to display to the screen, you would see the monitor display a half-drawn image as it refreshes while you're still drawing. This is commonly known as **screen tearing**.

To get around this, the concept of a **swap chain** was created. A swap chain is a series of textures that the monitor can iterate through, giving you time to draw the frame before the monitor needs to display it. Often, this is accomplished with just two texture buffers known as a **front buffer** and a **back buffer**. The front buffer is what the monitor will display while you draw to the Back Buffer. When you're finished rendering, the buffers are swapped so that the monitor can display the new frame and Direct3D can begin drawing the next frame; this is known as **double buffering**.

Sometimes two buffers are not enough; for example, when the monitor is still displaying the previous frame and Direct3D is ready to swap the buffers. This means that the API needs to wait for the monitor to finish displaying the previous frame before it can swap the buffers and let your game continue.

Alternatively, the API may discard the content that was just rendered, allowing the game to continue, but wasting a frame and causing the front buffer to repeat if the monitor wants to refresh while the game is drawing. This is where three buffers can come in handy, allowing the game to continue working and render ahead.

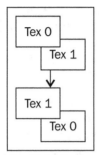

Double buffering

The swap chain is also directly tied to the resolution, and if the display area is resized, the swap chain needs to be recreated. You may think that all the games are full screen now and should not need to be resized! Remember that the snap functionality in Windows 8 resizes the screen, requiring your game to match the available space. Alongside the creation code, we need a way to respond to the window resize events so that we can resize the swap chain and elegantly handle the changes.

All of this happens inside `Direct3DBase::CreateWindowSizeDependentResources`. Here we will check to see if there is a resize, as well as some orientation-handling checks so that the game can handle rotation if enabled. We want to avoid the work that we don't need to do, and one of the benefits of Direct3D 11.1 is the ability to just resize the buffers in the swap chain. However, the really important code here executes if we do not already have a swap chain.

Many parts of Direct3D rely on creating a description structure that contains the information required to create the device, and then pass that information to a `Create()` method that will handle the rest of the creation. In this case, we will make use of a `DXGI_SWAP_CHAIN_DESC1` structure to describe the swap chain. The following code snippet shows what our structure will look like:

```
swapChainDesc.Width = static_cast<UINT>(m_renderTargetSize.Width);
swapChainDesc.Height = static_cast<UINT>(m_renderTargetSize.Height);
swapChainDesc.Format = DXGI_FORMAT_B8G8R8A8_UNORM;
```

```
swapChainDesc.Stereo = false;
swapChainDesc.SampleDesc.Count = 1;
swapChainDesc.SampleDesc.Quality = 0;
swapChainDesc.BufferUsage = DXGI_USAGE_RENDER_TARGET_OUTPUT;
swapChainDesc.BufferCount = 2;
swapChainDesc.Scaling = DXGI_SCALING_NONE;
swapChainDesc.SwapEffect = DXGI_SWAP_EFFECT_FLIP_SEQUENTIAL;
```

There are a lot of new concepts here, so let's work through each option one by one.

The `Width` and `Height` properties are self-explanatory; these come directly from the `CoreWindow` instance so that we can render at native resolution. If you want to force a different resolution, this would be where you specify that resolution.

The `Format` defines the layout of the pixels in the texture. Textures are represented as an array of colors, which can be packed in many different ways. The most common way is to lay out the different color channels in a `B8G8R8A8` format. This means that the pixel will have a single byte for each channel: Blue, Green, Red, and Alpha, in that order. The `UNORM` tells the system to store each pixel as an unsigned normalized integer. Put together, this forms `DXGI_FORMAT_B8G8R8A8_UNORM`.

The BGRA pixel layout

Often, the `R8G8B8A8` pixel layout is also used, however, both are well-supported and you can choose either.

The next flag, `Stereo`, tells the API if you want to take advantage of the Stereoscopic Rendering support in Direct3D 11.1. This is an advanced topic that we won't cover, so leave this as `false` for now.

The `SampleDesc` substructure describes our multisampling setting. Multisampling refers to a technique, commonly known as **MSAA** or **Multisample antialiasing**. Antialiasing refers to a technique that is used to reduce the sharp, jagged edges on polygons that arise from trying to map a line to the pixels when the line crosses through the middle of the pixel. MSAA resolves this by sampling within the pixel and filtering those values to get a nice average that represents detail smaller than a pixel. With antialiasing you will see nice smooth lines, at the cost of extra rendering and filtering. For our purposes, we will specify a single count, and zero quality, which tells the API to disable MSAA.

The `BufferUsage` enumeration tells the API how we plan to use the swap chain, which lets it make performance optimizations. This is most commonly used when creating normal textures, and should be left alone for now.

The `Scaling` parameter defines how the back buffer will be scaled if the texture resolution does not match the resolution that the operating system is providing to the monitor. You only have two options here: `DXGI_SCALING_STRETCH` and `DXGI_SCALING_NONE`.

The `SwapEffect` describes what happens when a swap between the front buffer and the back buffer(s) occurs. We're building a Windows Store application, so we only have one option here: `DXGI_SWAP_EFFECT_FLIP_SEQUENTIAL`. If we were building a desktop application, we would have a larger selection, and our final choice would depend on our performance and hardware requirements.

Now you may be wondering what **DXGI** is, and why we have been using it during the swap chain creation. Beginning with Windows Vista and Direct3D 10.0, the **DirectX Graphics Infrastructure (DXGI)** exists to act as an intermediary between the Direct3D API and the graphics driver. It manages the adapters and common graphics resources, as well as the Desktop Window Manager, which handles compositing multiple Direct3D applications together to allow multiple windows to share the same screen. DXGI manages the screen, and therefore manages the swap chain as well. That is why we have an `ID3D11Device` and an `IDXGISwapChain` object.

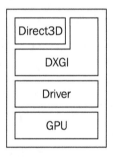

Once we're done, we need to use this structure to create the swap chain. You may remember, the graphics device creates resources, and that includes the swap chain. The swap chain, however, is a DXGI resource and not a Direct3D resource, so we first need to extract the DXGI device from the Direct3D device before we can continue. Thankfully, the Direct3D device is layered on top of the DXGI device, so we just need to convert the `ID3D11Device1` to an `IDXGIDevice1` with the following piece of code:

```
ComPtr<IDXGIDevice1> dxgiDevice;
DX::ThrowIfFailed(m_d3dDevice.As(&dxgiDevice));
```

Then we can get the adapter that the device is linked to, and the factory that serves the adapter, with the following code snippet:

```
ComPtr<IDXGIAdapter> dxgiAdapter;
DX::ThrowIfFailed(
  dxgiDevice->GetAdapter(&dxgiAdapter));

ComPtr<IDXGIFactory2> dxgiFactory;
DX::ThrowIfFailed(
  dxgiAdapter->GetParent(
    __uuidof(IDXGIFactory2),
    &dxgiFactory
    ));
```

Using the `IDXGIFactory2`, we can create the `IDXGISwapChain` that is tied to the adapter.

The 1 and 2 at the end of `IDXGIDevice1` and `IDXGIFactory2` differentiate between the different versions of Direct3D and DXGI that exist. Direct3D 11.1 is an add-on to Direct3D 11.0, so we need a way to define the different versions. The same goes for DXGI, which has gone through multiple versions since Vista.

```
dxgiFactory->CreateSwapChainForCoreWindow(
  m_d3dDevice.Get(),
  reinterpret_cast<IUnknown*>(window),
  &swapChainDesc,
  nullptr,
  &m_swapChain
  );
```

When we create the swap chain, we need to use a specific method for Windows Store applications, which takes the `CoreWindow` instance that we received when we created the application as a parameter. This would be where you pass a `HWND` Window handle, if you were using the old Win32 API. These handles let Direct3D connect the resource to the correct window and ensure that it is positioned properly when composited with the other windows on the screen.

Now we have a swap chain, almost ready for rendering. While we still have the DXGI device, we can also let it know that we want to enable a power-saving mode that ensures only one frame is queued up for display at a time.

```
dxgiDevice->SetMaximumFrameLatency(1);
```

This is especially important in Windows Store applications, as your game may be running on a mobile device, and your players wouldn't want to suddenly lose a lot of battery rendering frames that they do not need.

Render target, depth stencil, and viewport

The next step is to get a reference to the back buffer in the swap chain, so that we can make use of it later on. First, we need to get the back buffer texture from the swap chain, which can be easily done with a call to the `GetBuffer()` method. This will give us a pointer to a texture buffer, which we can use to create a render target view, as follows:

```
ComPtr<ID3D11Texture2D> backBuffer;
  m_swapChain->GetBuffer(
    0,
    __uuidof(ID3D11Texture2D),
    &backBuffer
    );
```

Direct3D 10 and later versions provide access to the different graphics resources using constructs called **views**. These let us tell the API how to use the resource, and provide a way of accessing the resources after creation.

In the following code snippet we are creating a **render target view** (`ID3D11RenderTargetView`), which, as the name implies, provides a view into a render target. If you haven't encountered the term before, a **render target** is a texture that you can draw into, for use later. This allows us to draw to **off-screen textures**, which we can then use in many different ways to create the final rendered frame.

```
m_d3dDevice->CreateRenderTargetView(
    backBuffer.Get(),
    nullptr,
    &m_renderTargetView
    )
```

Now that we have a render target view, we can tell the graphics context to use this as the back buffer and start drawing, but while we're initializing our graphics let's create a depth buffer texture and view so that we can have some depth in our game.

A depth buffer is a special texture that is responsible for storing the depth of each pixel on the screen. This can be used by the GPU to quickly cull pixels that are hidden by other objects. Being able to avoid drawing objects that we cannot see is important, as drawing those objects still takes time, even though they do not contribute to the scene. Previously, I mentioned that we need to draw a frame in a small amount of time to achieve certain frame rates.

In complex games, this can be difficult to achieve if we are drawing everything, so culling is important to ensure that we can achieve the performance we want.

The depth buffer is an optional feature that isn't automatically generated with the swap chain, so we need to create it ourselves. To do this, we need to describe the texture we want to create with a `D3D11_TEXTURE2D_DESC` structure. Direct3D 11.1 provides a nice helper structure in the form of a `CD3D11_TEXTURE2D_DESC` that handles filling in common values for us, as follows:

```
CD3D11_TEXTURE2D_DESC depthStencilDesc(
  DXGI_FORMAT_D24_UNORM_S8_UINT,
  static_cast<UINT>(m_renderTargetSize.Width),
  static_cast<UINT>(m_renderTargetSize.Height),
  1,
  1,
  D3D11_BIND_DEPTH_STENCIL
  );
```

Here we're asking for a texture that has a pixel format of 24 bits for the depth, in an unsigned normalized integer, and 8 bits for the stencil in an unsigned integer. The Stencil part of this buffer is an advanced feature that lets you assign a value to pixels in the texture. This is most often used for creating a mask, and support is provided for only rendering to regions with a specific stencil value.

After this, we will set the width and height to match the swap chain, and fill in the **Array Size** and **Mip Levels** so that we can reach the parameter that lets us describe the usage of the texture. The Array Size refers to the number of textures to create. If you want an array of textures combined as a single resource, you can use this parameter to specify the count, but we only want one texture, so we will set this to 1.

Mip Levels are increasingly smaller textures that match the main texture. This is used to allow for performance optimizations when rendering the texture at a distance where the original resolution is overkilled. For example, say you have a screen resolution of 800 by 600. If you want three Mip levels, you will receive an 800 x 600 texture, a 400 x 300 texture, and a 200 x 150 texture. The graphics card has hardware to filter and must use the correct texture, thus reducing the amount of wastage involved in rendering. Our depth buffer here will never be rendered at a distance, so we don't need to use up extra memory providing different Mip Levels; we will just set this to 1 to say that we only want the original resolution texture.

Finally, we will tell the structure that we want this texture to be bound as a depth stencil. This lets the driver make optimizations to ensure that this special texture can be quickly accessed where needed. We round this out by creating the texture using the following description structure:

```
m_d3dDevice->CreateTexture2D(
  &depthStencilDesc,
  nullptr,
  &depthStencil
  )
```

Now that we have a depth buffer texture, we need a **depth stencil view** (ID3D11DepthStencilView) to bind it, as with our render target earlier. We will use another description structure for it (CD3D11_DEPTH_STENCIL_VIEW_DESC). However, we can get away with just a single parameter and the type of texture; in this case it is a D3D11_DSV_DIMENSION_TEXTURE2D. We can then create the view, ready for use, as shown:

```
m_d3dDevice->CreateDepthStencilView(
    depthStencil.Get(),
    &depthStencilViewDesc,
    &m_depthStencilView
    )
```

Now that we have a device, context, swap chain, render target, and depth buffer, we just need to describe one more thing before we're ready to kick off the game loop. The **viewport** describes the layout of the area we want to render. In most cases, you will just define the full size of the render target here; however, some situations may need you to draw to just a small section of the screen, maybe for a split screen mode. The viewport lets you define the region once and render as normal for that region, and then define a new viewport for the new region so you can render into it.

To create this viewport, we just need to specify the x and y coordinates of the top-left corner, as well as the width and height of the viewport. We want to use the entire screen, so our top-left corner is x = 0, y = 0, and our width and height match our render target, as shown:

```
CD3D11_VIEWPORT viewport(
    0.0f,
    0.0f,
    m_renderTargetSize.Width,
    m_renderTargetSize.Height
    );

m_d3dContext->RSSetViewports(1, &viewport);
```

Now that we have created everything, we just need to finish up by setting the render target view and depth stencil view so that the API knows to use them. This is done with a single call to the `m_d3dContext->OMSetRenderTargets()` method, passing the number of render targets, a pointer to the first render target view pointer, and a pointer to the depth stencil view.

Down the graphics pipeline

Let's step aside for a moment to understand the stages that the graphics card goes through when it renders something to the screen, also called the **graphics pipeline**.

To do this, we need to understand what exactly is drawn to the screen, even when we're just working in 2D. The base component of something drawn onto the screen is a **vertex**. The vertex is a point in space, that, when combined with at least two other points, forms a solid triangle that can be rendered. By combining multiple triangles together, you can create anything from a simple square to a detailed 3D model with thousands of triangles.

Often, vertices will share the same space, so we need a way to reduce the repetition and memory use by only defining a vertex once. However, how do we indicate which triangles use this vertex? This is where the **index** enters. Just as with arrays, the index allows you to map to a particular vertex using much less memory. This way you can have a lot of data per vertex, and reference a single vertex multiple times by defining the triangles with an array of indices.

How does all this get mapped and calculated so that we render the right thing? This is where the **Input Assembler (IA)** comes into play. The IA takes the vertex and index buffers (arrays) and builds a list of triangle vertices that need to be drawn. These are then passed to the **vertex shader**.

The vertex shader is a piece of code that we use to map the 3D position of a vertex to its 2D position on the screen. We'll be using DirectXTK for this so we can avoid worrying about vertex shaders for now; however if you want to start adding awesome visual features and take advantage of the hardware, you will want to learn about these shaders. Vertex shaders are written in a language called the **High Level Shader Language (HLSL)**.

Once we have a transformed vertex, we can take advantage of some new Direct3D 10.0 and Direct3D 11.0 features: the **tessellation shader** and the **geometry shader**.

Tessellation refers to the act of increasing geometric detail by adding more triangles. This is done through two different shaders, the **hull shader** and the **domain shader**. Tessellation is an advanced topic that is too big for this book. I encourage you to take a look at the many resources available online if you're interested in this topic.

Geometry shaders were introduced in Direct3D 10.0, and provide a way to generate geometry completely on the GPU. These allow for some interesting tricks; however, they're also well outside the scope of this book, so we'll skip over them for now. The hull, domain, and geometry shaders are optional features that are not available on pre-Direct3D 10.0 hardware.

Once we have processed the vertices, they are sent to the **rasterizer**, which is responsible for interpolating across the screen and finding the region of pixels that represent the object. This happens automatically and results in the input to the **pixel shader**.

The pixel shader is where the final color of the pixel is determined. Here, we can apply lighting effects to generate the photorealistic scenes we see in modern games, or anything else that we want. In the pixel shader stage, the developer has full control over the final look, which can result in some crazy visual effects, as evident in the many demoscene projects that are created each year.

> The demoscene is a collection of developers who create visual experiences, often set to music, and in incredibly small executables. It's easy to find demo challenges that require a maximum executable size of 64k or even 4k.

Finally, we will end up with a lot of pixels, some even trying to share the same spot on the texture. This is where the **Output Merger** combines everything down into a flat 2D texture that can be displayed on the screen. The Output Merger handles resolving the pixels down to a single color and writing them out to our render target and depth buffer.

Understanding the game loop

The core of our game happens in the **game loop**. This is where all of the logic and subsystems are processed, and the frame is rendered, many times per second. The game loop consists of two major actions: **updating** and **drawing**.

Updating the simulation

Now we can get to the action. A game is a simulation of a world, and just like a movie simulates motion by displaying multiple frames per second, games simulate a living world by advancing the simulation many times per second, each time stopping to draw a view into the current state of the game world.

The simplest update will just advance the timer, which is provided to us through the `BasicTimer` class. The timer keeps track of the amount of time that has elapsed since the previous frame, or since the timer was started — usually the start of the game. Keeping track of the time is important because we need the **frame delta** (time since the last frame) to correctly advance the simulation by just the right amount. We also work at a millisecond level, sometimes even a fraction of a millisecond, so we need to make use of the floating point data types to appropriately track these values.

Once the time has been updated, most games will accept and parse player input, as this often has the most important effect on the world. Doing this before the rest of the processing means you can act on input immediately rather than delaying by a frame. The amount of time between an input by the player and a reaction in the game world appearing on screen is called **latency**. Many games that require fast input need to reduce or eliminate latency to ensure the player has a great experience. High latency can make the game feel sluggish or laggy, and frustrate players.

Once we've processed the time and input, we need to process everything else required to make the game world seem alive. This can include (but is not limited to) the following:

- Physics
- Networking
- Artificial Intelligence
- Gameplay
- Pathfinding
- Audio

Drawing the world

Once we have an up-to-date game world, we need to display a view of the world to the players so that they can receive some kind of feedback for their actions. This is done during the draw stage, which can either be the cheapest or most expensive part of the frame, depending on what you want to render.

The `Draw()` method (sometimes also called the `Render()` method) is commonly broken down into three sections: clearing the screen, drawing the world, and presenting the frame to the monitor for display.

Clearing the screen

During the rendering of each frame, the same render target is reused. Just like any data, it remains there unless we clear it away before trying to make use of the texture. Clearing the screen is paramount if you use a depth buffer. If you do not clear the depth buffer, the old data will be used and can prevent certain visuals from rendering when they should, as the GPU believes that something has already been drawn in front.

Clearing the render target and depth buffer allows us to reinitialize the data in each pixel to a clean value, ready for use in the new frame.

To clear both the buffers we need to issue two commands, one for each. This is the first time we will use the views that we created earlier. Using our ID3D11DeviceContext, we will call both the ClearRenderTargetView() and ClearDepthStencilView() methods to clear the buffers. For the first method you need to pass a color that will be set across the buffer. In most cases setting black (0, 0, 0, 1 in RGBA) will be enough; however, you may want to set a different color for debug purposes, which you can do here with a simple float array.

Clearing the depth just needs a single floating point value, in this case 1.0f, which represents the farthest distance from the camera. Data in the depth buffer is represented by values between 0 and 1, with 0 being the closest to the camera. We also need to tell the command which parts of the depth buffer we want to clear. We won't use the stencil buffer, so we will just clear the depth buffer using D3D11_CLEAR_DEPTH, and leave the default of 0 for the stencil value.

The auto keyword is a new addition to C++ in the C++11 specification. It allows the compiler to determine the data type, instead of requiring the programmer to specify it explicitly.

```
auto rtvs = m_renderTargetView.Get();
m_d3dContext->OMSetRenderTargets(
1,
&rtvs,
m_depthStencilView.Get()
);
const float clearCol[4] = { 0.0f, 0.0f, 0.0f, 1.0f };
m_d3dContext->ClearRenderTargetView(
  rtvs,
  clearCol
  );
m_d3dContext->ClearDepthStencilView(
  m_depthStencilView.Get(),
```

```
D3D11_CLEAR_DEPTH,
1.0f,
0);
```

You'll notice that aside from clearing the depth buffer, we're also setting some render targets at the start. This is because in Windows 8 the render target is unbound when we present the frame, so at the start of the new frame we need to rebind the render target so that the GPU has somewhere to draw to.

Now that we have a clean slate, we can start rendering the world. We'll get into this in the next chapter, but this is where we will draw our textures onto the screen to create the world. The user interface is also drawn at this point, and once this stage is complete you should end up with the finished frame, ready for display.

Presenting the back buffer

Once we have a frame ready to display, we need to tell Direct3D that we are done drawing and it can flip the back buffer with the front buffer. To do this we tell the API to **present** the frame.

When we present the frame, we can indicate to DXGI that it should wait until the next **vertical retrace** before swapping the buffers. The vertical retrace is the period of time where the monitor is not refreshing the screen. It comes from the days of CRT monitors where the electron beam would return to the top of the screen to start displaying a new frame.

We previously looked at tearing, and how it can impact the visual quality of the game. To fix this issue we use **VSync**. Try turning off VSync in a modern game and watch for lines in the display where the frame is broken by the new frame.

Another thing we can do when we present is define a region that has changed, so that we do not waste power updating all of the screen when only part of it has changed. If you're working on a game you probably won't need this; however, many other Direct3D applications only need to update part of the screen and this can be a useful optimization in an increasing mobile and low-power world.

To get started, we need to define a DXGI_PRESENT_PARAMETERS structure in which we will define the region that we want to present, as follows:

```
DXGI_PRESENT_PARAMETERS parameters = {0};
parameters.DirtyRectsCount = 0;
parameters.pDirtyRects = nullptr;
parameters.pScrollRect = nullptr;
parameters.pScrollOffset = nullptr;
```

In this case we want to clear the entire screen, so Direct3D lets us indicate that by presenting with zero dirty regions.

Now we can commit by using the `Present1()` method in the swap chain:

```
m_swapChain->Present1(1, 0, &parameters);
```

The first parameter defines the sync interval, and this is where you would enable or disable VSync. The interval can be any positive integer, and refers to how many refreshes should complete before the swap occurs. A value of zero here will result in VSync being disabled, while a value of one would lock the presentation rate to the monitor refresh rate. You can also use a value above one, which will result in the refresh rate being divided by the provided interval. For example, if you have a monitor with a 60 Hz refresh rate, a value of one would present at 60 Hz, while a value of two would present at 30 Hz.

At this point, we've done everything we need to initialize and render a frame; however, you'll notice the generated code adds some more lines, as shown in the following code snippet:

```
m_d3dContext->DiscardView(m_renderTargetView.Get());

m_d3dContext->DiscardView(m_depthStencilView.Get());
```

These two lines allow the driver to apply some optimizations by hinting that we will not be using the contents of the back buffer after this frame. You can get away with not including these lines if you want, but it doesn't hurt to add them and maybe reap the benefits later.

Summary

Now you should understand how to get started with a basic Direct3D 11.1 application in Windows 8. We've covered the creation of the application, including how to create the new modern window, and how to initialize Direct3D with all of its individual parts.

We have also covered the graphics pipeline; how each stage works together to produce the final image. From there we looked at all of the components we created, such as the device, context, swap chain, render target, and depth stencil. We then looked at how to apply those to start creating frames to display. By clearing the screen, we ensured that there is a fresh slate for the images and effects we want to draw later, and then we presented those frames, looking at how to specify regions of the screen to optimize for performance when you only change part of the screen.

Next steps

Now we have a running Direct3D app that displays a nice single color (or nothing at all), ready to start rendering textures and other objects onto the screen. In the next chapter we'll start drawing images and text to the screen before we can move on to creating a game.

This chapter skipped over some smaller topics such as lost devices and the correct way to resize the screen; however, the generated code provides all of this. I'd encourage you to take a look at the rest of the code in `Direct3DBase.cpp`; it has plenty of comments to help you understand the rest of the code.

2
Drawing 2D Sprites

Some newer independent games make use of only audio or other feedback systems to convey the game state to he player; however, most games still use the tried and true method of showing the game to the user through a graphical representation. To really get started, we need to be able to put something onto the screen for the player. In this chapter we will do just that. We'll look at how to load the images from files on disk, and then display them on the screen, in 2D through a 3D API.

One of the best things you can do to make your life easier when writing code is rely on the efforts of others before you. Many thousands of people have written 2D rendering algorithms before this book was even written, and their learnings and efforts should not be wasted by scrapping all of that information and starting from scratch. Microsoft provides an open source library that tries to collect this information and give you a head start in developing your game. **DirectXTK** is a small library designed to do all of these common tasks for you. We'll be using this to simplify the task of loading textures from disk, rendering them onto the screen, and working with fonts to display some text on the screen.

Through the course of this chapter we will add the ability to draw images and text. We'll start by learning how to load in textures and draw them to the screen using DirectXTK. After that, we will look at text rendering and how to add that functionality to the game for future use. By the end of the chapter, you should have some images and text on screen, ready for gameplay.

In this chapter you will:

- Download and build DirectXTK
- Learn about sprites and textures
- Understand co-ordinate spaces and projections
- Learn about texture formats

- Discover how to load textures
- Draw some sprites to the screen
- Learn about text rendering
- Render some text to the screen

Installing DirectXTK

We will use NuGet, a development package manager that comes with Visual Studio 2012 to install DirectXTK. Before this can happen, we need to ensure it is up-to-date using the **Extensions and Updates** dialog, found in the **Tools** menu. (Select **Updates** on the left side of the dialog.) Once it is up-to-date, we can use NuGet to install C++ packages. Right-click on your game project in Visual Studio and choose **Manage NuGet packages**. This will bring up the management dialog, where we can search for new packages. Search for `DirectXTK` and install the DirectX Tool Kit when it appears.

Once it finishes downloading, it will integrate with your project, allowing you to include any of the header files using the `#include <file.h>` directive.

If you want further information about the toolkit, visit `http://directxtk. codeplex.com`, which will let you access the source code as well as the feature list for the library. For this project we will only be using the following types:

- `SpriteBatch`
- `SpriteFont`

Most of the other features relate to 3D games and can be ignored.

What a sprite is

Sprites and **textures** are pretty similar, but their differences appear when you look at what they do when the game is running. A texture is quite simply a 2D image that we can generate or load from the disk. In many cases, sprites are the same as textures, and you won't need to worry about them. Technically though, a sprite is a runtime representation of the image within the context of the game scene. This is because we can use parts of the texture (or multiple textures) as a sprite, giving the illusion of a complete image coming from a single texture. The difference really appears when you have sprite sheet-based animations (animations with each frame arrayed on the same texture).

Sprites were originally images that sat on top of the frame buffer, seemingly integrated into the bitmap even though they were just layered on top. These days sprites just refer to individual images displayed to the player.

When you look at an animation, you will see a series of frames displayed in rapid sequence, giving the illusion of movement. Often these frames are packed together on a single texture, also known as a sprite sheet. The texture is always the full image with all frames; however, when displayed within the context of the game, only single frames are drawn, and this display of frames as a single object is called the sprite.

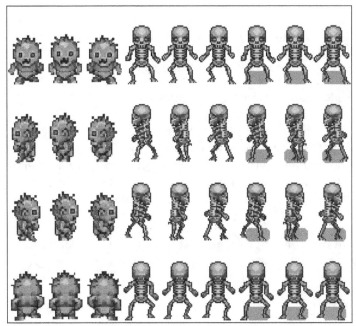

Example Sprite Sheet
Credits: Reemax & artisticdude

Sprites can range from representing the player or enemies with animations, to static objects that fill the entire background. Sprites may be rotated, scaled, moved, or even layered with other sprites, allowing for on the fly positioning and customization.

Textures

Textures store the image data we need to display on the screen. They represent a 2D array of pixels in memory that can be used for many different purposes, as you will see in this book.

The pixels inside a texture are referred to as **texels**. We use this distinction because through filtering, scaling, and other transformations, we may lose the 1:1 mapping between a texel in the image and a pixel in the output frame buffer.

Textures also take up much of the memory available to a game, making it important that you apply techniques to reduce their size as much as possible when working on memory limited devices such as tablets or phones. Textures are generally stored on the GPU in special memory designed for quick access; however, on some platforms that memory is shared with the system memory, reducing the amount of space you have even further.

GPU refers **to Graphics Processing Unit**. This is a piece of acceleration hardware that is designed to handle the mathematics required to create our game images at the rates required for an interactive game. The focus on rendering allows the hardware to be specialised and perform better than a CPU for rendering tasks.

Textures are static; however, by using a texture as a sprite sheet you can add animation to your game and reduce the number of files you need to load. Textures themselves do not define anything but the format of the pixel in memory, the width, and the height, leaving the interpretation and use up to you. We won't go into detail about these techniques, but there is plenty of information available online if you want to add animations to your game.

Now let's look at the different formats that we can use, and load them in ready for rendering later on.

File formats

There are many different image file formats; however, we'll focus on two major formats in use today:

* PNG
* DXT (Uses the `.dds` extension)

PNG is a well-known format, widely used online for images. It can be read by most editing programs and has plenty of ways to load and decode the image from the file. It supports features such as transparency and provides reasonable lossless compression, making it an excellent choice for storing and editing images in lieu of a format such as **Photoshop Document (PSD)**.

DXT on the other hand was created for rendering 3D textured images, and achieved popularity when included in both Direct3D and OpenGL. As a result DXT has many benefits that other image formats lack when used in a game. The first and foremost benefit is the native support on GPUs for decoding and decompressing the format. Instead of having to load in and use the CPU to do these operations, you just need to read the file in and send it to the GPU, which can handle the rest. This greatly simplifies the content load process, and improves efficiency by reducing the amount of memory and processing time needed.

[A DXT texture converter, `texconv.exe`, is included with the source code for this chapter.]

Loading

First we need to ensure the images are packaged with the game when we create our builds for testing and for the store. To do this, we need to add the image to the project, and ensure that the **Content** property is set to **true**. This is done through the **Properties** window in Visual Studio. The simplest way to open it if it is not already open is to select the texture file in your solution explorer and press *F4*. Inside the properties inspector (with the file selected) you will see a **Content** property, which you can change to **true**. Once that is done, the images will be included, and will be ready for use.

We want to load two different textures onto the screen for this exercise:

- `player.dds`
- `enemy.dds`

To begin, we'll need to create something to hold and manage these images, so create a `Texture` class. In the sample, I've created a `Texture` class using the new C++/CX ref class system so that I can get the benefit of automatic reference counting and resource management. You can use a standard C++ class here, but you need to ensure that you manage the allocation and cleanup, either manually or using smart pointers.

Inside `Texture.h`, place the following code:

```
#pragma once
#include <SpriteBatch.h>

ref class Texture sealed
{
private:
  Platform::String^ _path;
```

```
    Microsoft::WRL::ComPtr<ID3D11Texture2D> _tex;
    Microsoft::WRL::ComPtr<ID3D11ShaderResourceView> _srv;
    DirectX::XMFLOAT2 _pos;

  internal:
    void Load(Microsoft::WRL::ComPtr<ID3D11Device> device);

  public:
    property float X
    {
      float get() { return _pos.x; }
      void set(float val) { _pos.x = val; }
    }
    property float Y
    {
      float get() { return _pos.y; }
      void set(float val) { _pos.y = val; }
    }
    Texture(Platform::String^ path);
};
```

Here we're defining a simple `Texture` class that has properties for the co-ordinates of the texture and a way to load the texture. We need to use internal visibility because DirectXTK is implemented as a set of standard C++ classes, and therefore can't be exposed to WinRT. By using the internal modifier we can limit access to the `Load` method from code within the same assembly, allowing us to use standard pointers in a WinRT (ref) class, which does not allow standard C++ pointers to be exposed publicly.

Inside `Texture.cpp`, we want to define a constructor that sets the _path field and then define the `Load` method, as follows:

```
void Texture::Load(Microsoft::WRL::ComPtr<ID3D11Device> device)
{
  DirectX::CreateDDSTextureFromFile(
    device.Get(),
    _path->Data(),
    &_tex,
    &_srv
  );
}
```

Make sure you include the header file `DDSTextureLoader.h` from DirectXTK for this to work.

In the preceding code, we're simply calling a nice and handy helper function that is designed to load the `.dds` file and create the required D3D11 resources, ready for use. We let that method directly set the `ID3D11Resource` and `ID3D11ShaderResourceView` in our class.

Now we need to load in the textures that we added to the project earlier. We're going to be managing the game inside our `Game` class (the one that implements `Direct3DBase`). For now we'll start by adding in the two textures, and loading them up. Later on we'll create a manager to handle these textures and clean up the code.

Start by including `Texture.h` in your `Game` header, and add the following fields to that class:

```
Texture^ _player;
Texture^ _enemy;
```

Now we need to create a place to load this content. Let's add a `LoadContent` method to our `Game` class, and then let's call `Initialize` in `GameApplication` and invoke `LoadContent`.

Now create the following in our new `LoadContent` method:

```
void Game::LoadContent()
{
  _player = ref new Texture("textures\\player.dds");
  _enemy = ref new Texture("textures\\enemy.dds");

  _player->X = 50;
  _player->Y = 50;

  _enemy->X = 300;
  _enemy->Y = 300;

  _player->Load(m_d3dDevice);
  _enemy->Load(m_d3dDevice);
}
```

This is all pretty straightforward. We create the textures, and place the player and enemy in different positions so they have some clear space to draw, and then we tell the game to actually proceed and load the textures.

Feel free to test the project. You won't see anything on screen but if the game loads and starts clearing the screen like it did in the previous chapter then everything should be fine so far.

Co-ordinate systems

We're using Direct3D to display our 2D world, which means we need to consider the differences between how we work with 3D and what we need for 2D, and adapt to make everything fit together. For our purposes DirectXTK will take care of most of this; however it's useful to know what's going on, and understand the concepts involved so that you can delve into advanced concepts in future to create some amazing visuals.

In 2D the world is represented as a **Cartesian** plane, with the X-axis representing the horizontal axis, and the Y-axis representing the vertical. Many 2D systems, including Direct3D and DirectXTK, position the co-ordinate (0, 0), also known as the **origin**, at the top-left corner of the screen.

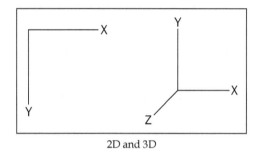

2D and 3D

3D adds a third dimension, Z, to the mix, which represents the axis perpendicular to both X and Y, heading "away" from the viewer if you view the X/Y plane head on. When referring to the camera, this represents the depth of the image, and can be translated to the 2D world to add layering and depth between the flat images.

This brings us to another topic — **cameras**. A camera is a virtual representation of real life cameras; they handle defining what is actually rendered on screen, and where, allowing for us to easily move the view around without messing with the entire game world.

You may be used to cameras in 3D games that have perspective (objects get smaller, the further away they are). A projection is the transformation from a 3D world to a flat 2D world, which is often called screen space. A **perspective** projection allows us to turn the lines and shapes of the world into a flat image that conveys depth by angling lines towards the horizon to introduce perspective.

A cube in perspective (left) and orthographic (right) projections

The problem with using the perspective projection for 2D is that we may want our sprites to look 3D, but they contain no depth information. When rendered with sprites sitting behind them, they will look mismatched and wrong. This is where the **Orthographic** projection comes into play. An orthographic projection prevents perspective from entering the image and allows us to control the illusion of the depth in a way that fits with the 2D sprites we are using.

Drawing the sprites

Now we need to get those images onto the screen. Using DirectXTK we have access to a class called `SpriteBatch`. If you have used XNA before, you might recognize this class and remember that it is an excellent way to render 2D images with all of the effort and optimization done for you.

For this we need to prepare the `SpriteBatch` inside our `Game` class so we can render the textures we have created, and then from there add some code to the `Texture` class so that we can finally draw these images.

Let's begin by defining a shared pointer to a `SpriteBatch` object within the `Game` class. Remember that DirectXTK defines all of its classes within the DirectX namespace, so you'll need to create something like the following:

```
std::shared_ptr<DirectX::SpriteBatch> _spriteBatch;
```

Once you've done that, we need to create `SpriteBatch`. This requires a device context so that it can create the required internal resources. Add the following line to the start of your `LoadContent` method within the `Game` class.

```
Microsoft::WRL::ComPtr<ID3D11DeviceContext> d3d11DeviceContext;
m_d3dContext.As(&d3d11DeviceContext);
_spriteBatch = std::make_shared<DirectX::SpriteBatch>(
    d3d11DeviceContext.Get()
);
```

Here we need to convert the device context we have from `ID3D11DeviceContext1` to `ID3D11DeviceContext`. The `ComPtr` type allows us to do this easily, and once we have that we can create `SpriteBatch`.

Now we have a working `SpriteBatch` that can be used to render our textures. The next step is to draw the sprites. We're using `SpriteBatch` and, as the name implies, the sprites will be drawn batched together. This improves performance by giving the GPU a nice chunk of work to do in a minimal number of API calls, so we don't need to keep going through the API and driver layers continuously, wasting time. To do this, we need to let the batch know when it should begin and when we're done issuing the commands, so that it can do some work, batch everything together, and draw to the screen.

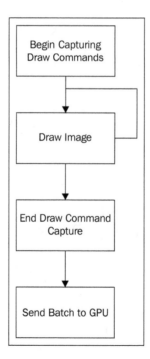

To do this, we need to call `SpriteBatch->Begin()` before we draw anything. For our purposes, we can just call `Begin` without any parameters; however, if you want to alter the GPU state during the batch, or change the batching mode, you would do that here.

Sorting modes

There are a few different modes available for batching, so you can choose the best one for your situation:

- `SpriteSortMode_Deferred`
- `SpriteSortMode_Immediate`
- `SpriteSortMode_FrontToBack`
- `SpriteSortMode_BackToFront`
- `SpriteSortMode_Texture`

`Deferred` is the default option, and this takes the sprites in the order you submit them, waits until `End` is called, and then submits them to be drawn.

`Immediate` removes the benefit of batching by sending draw calls for every sprite you draw, as soon as you call `Draw`. This is useful in some cases where batching is giving you issues or you just want to use `SpriteBatch` as an easy way to do 2D.

`FrontToBack` sorts the sprites by their depth parameter, drawing the sprites closest to the screen (0.0f) first. `BackToFront` does the opposite, and draws the sprites behind first. This is where you need to look at what you're drawing and make a decision. By rendering `FrontToBack` you make the most of the depth culling functionality on modern GPUs. As the closest sprites are drawn first, the GPU knows that those pixels are now occluded and minimizes overdraw in those regions. `BackToFront` is often necessary when you are working with transparent sprites, often in particle effects. To keep using depth culling with other objects, you need to render these back to front to ensure that the particles can blend together without artifacts.

Finally, texture is a special sorting mode, where the batch will look at the textures you're drawing and determine if you're reusing the same texture anywhere. If you are, it can batch the calls together for each texture, optimizing the number of texture swaps that need to occur, which can often be a major bottleneck for texture heavy games.

Finishing the batch

Now that we have begun rendering, we can draw each texture individually. To do this, we'll add a `Draw` method to our `Texture` class that will handle the rendering for you. Inside the `Texture` class header, declare the following method prototype under the `internal` modifier:

```
void Draw(std::shared_ptr<DirectX::SpriteBatch> batch);
```

Once you've done that, implement the method in the `.cpp` file by adding the following code:

```
void Texture::Draw(std::shared_ptr<DirectX::SpriteBatch> batch)
{
  auto vPos = DirectX::XMLoadFloat2(&_pos);
  batch->Draw(_srv.Get(), vPos, nullptr);
}
```

The main part of this method is the call to `batch->Draw()`, which tells the `SpriteBatch` to draw the texture, or save it for later (depending on which sort mode you chose).

We need to tell the `Draw` call where to place the sprite on the screen. This is done through the second parameter, which asks for an `FXMVECTOR` from the `DirectXMath` library that comes with Direct3D and Windows 8. To do this we will have to load our `_pos` variable, which is stored as `XMFLOAT2 (X, Y)`, into `XMVECTOR`, which can be passed to the `Draw` function.

After that, we will pass a `nullptr` value to the final parameter, which asks us to define which region of the texture should be drawn. Here we can define a sub-region of the texture and just draw that part; however, in our case we want to draw the whole thing, so to make that simpler we can pass a `nullptr` value and skip having to manually get the size of the texture and create a rectangle that defines the entire region.

Vectors

A vector can be simply described as an array of numbers, which in this case refer to a co-ordinate location on the 2D screen. In this book I will refer to vectors in the form (X, Y), where X and Y represent their respective co-ordinates.

DirectXMath provides plenty of helper functions and utilities to make working with vectors easy, and the `SimpleMath` library contained within DirectXTK makes this even easier.

So now we can finish rendering the sprites by calling the `Draw` function we just implemented for each of our sprites and then ending the batch. Return to the `Game` class' `Draw` method and add the following code after our `Clear` calls:

```
_spriteBatch->Begin();

_player->Draw(_spriteBatch);
_enemy->Draw(_spriteBatch);

_spriteBatch->End();
```

Here we're calling our new `Draw` method on each of the textures we created and loaded. After that we call `End` on the sprite batch, which informs it that we are done issuing commands and it can proceed with rendering.

Because we are using the default `Begin` method, we need to ensure that we specify the order in which these textures are drawn. One useful example is if you want to have a background in a game. If you draw the player and other objects before the background without any form of sorting, you will end up writing over the player images, and all you will see is the background. So ensure you check your draw order before actually drawing to the screen; and if you can't see some sprites that should be there, make sure you aren't hiding them accidentally.

Now run the game and you should see our two sprites rendered onto the screen, ready to come alive once we add some gameplay.

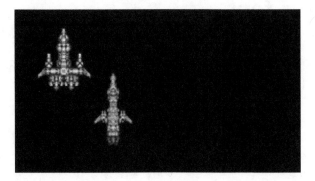

Text rendering

So now that we have some images rendering to the screen, you're ready to start making millions. But wait, how are you going to communicate with the player? If you are making an art game, you could probably get away with zero text, but most games need to communicate with the players so they have the information they need to play successfully. To do this, we need to render some text.

Windows has plenty of built in text functionality for rendering text in Windows 8 applications; however, we're working with raw Direct3D, so we don't have access to that, and in many cases those nice features would get in the way of our games.

Thankfully we don't need to worry about perfect kerning and other text features that are needed for a great reading experience, so text rendering becomes really easy. Add in the `SpriteFont` class from DirectXTK and you'll be subtitling everything before you know it.

TTF versus BMP

Many fonts these days are stored as something called a **True Type Font** (TTF). These define all of the details about the fonts and store them in a vector graphic form (not the same as vectors in the previous section) so that the operating system can render text in a crisp, correct fashion. Reading and correctly rendering these files is a complicated endeavour, and for many games the detail just isn't needed. Therefore we need another solution.

Enter the **bitmap font**. A bitmap font takes that detailed processing and does it all up front so we get a nice texture with every character we need rendered out. This way, rendering text is as simple as just drawing the part of the texture that contains the glyph you want, and doing this for every letter in the word or sentence.

Building the font

As I just mentioned, we need to process the original TTF font into a texture that we can use for rendering. Thankfully DirectXTK provides a command-line tool that will do this for us quickly and easily. If you're using NuGet, you can find a pre-compiled version of this tool in the following directory:

```
packages\directxtk<version number>\tools\native
```

`MakeSpriteFont.exe` can also be found with the source code for this chapter, as well as in source code form from the DirectXTK repository mentioned at the start of this chapter.

`MakeSpriteFont` has a number of configuration options that you can use to tailor your font file.

Parameter	Description
CharacterRegion	A region of characters to include in the font file, defined using hex notation. For example, /CharacterRegion:0x20-0x7F.
DefaultCharacter	The fallback character to render when your game requests a character that isn't in the font file. Defaults to throwing an exception.
FontSize	The size of the font, same as the font settings in any other program with fonts. Defaults to 23pt.
FontStyle	The style of the font; for example Italic or Bold. Defaults to Regular.
LineSpacing	Overrides the distances between adjacent lines. Negative values will reduce the spacing; positive values will increase the spacing.
CharacterSpacing	Similar to LineSpacing, but this alters the distance between adjacent characters.
TextureFormat	The pixel format of the output texture. The options are Auto, Rgba32, Bgra4444, and CompressedMono. Defaults to Auto, which usually gives CompressedMono to reduce file size.
NoPremultiply	Uses interpolative alpha instead of pre-multiplied alpha. Defaults to off/false.
DebugOutputSpriteSheet	Provides an image version of your sprite sheet so you can check the output.

For the example game, we'll generate a simple sprite font for the Segoe UI font that ships with Windows 8. Remember that when you add fonts to your game, you need to ensure you're licensed to distribute them with software.

Start a command prompt at the location of MakeSpriteFont.exe and run the following command:

```
MakeSpriteFont.exe "Segoe UI" "GameFont.font"
```

 To quickly open the command prompt in your current folder, hold *Shift* while you right-click and select **Open Command Prompt Here**.

This will output a file named GameFont.font, which we can include in our game as we did with the images previously. Don't forget to set the **Content** property to **true**.

Drawing the font

Now let's get this text onto the screen. The steps here are pretty simple, just like our sprite rendering before.

Inside the game we need to define a SpriteFont that will hold our font data and work with SpriteBatch to render the text. Add this underneath the SpriteBatch definition:

```
std::shared_ptr<DirectX::SpriteFont> _spriteFont;
```

Now we need to load this up using the constructor of SpriteFont. The best place to do this would be after loading the sprites inside the Game->Load() function.

```
Microsoft::WRL::ComPtr<ID3D11Device> d3d11Device;
m_d3dDevice.As(&d3d11Device);
_spriteFont = std::make_shared<DirectX::SpriteFont>(
  d3d11Device.Get(),
  L"GameFont.font"
);
```

Here we need to get the ID3D11Device version of our graphics device, and we only have the ID3D11Device1 version. So, just as with our earlier conversion of the device context, use the ComPtr type to help convert and give us a device we can use.

After that, we just need to provide that device, as well as a wchar_t path to our font file, relative to the application directory. In our case we are storing our font in the root game directory.

Now we have the font loaded and ready, and it is a simple matter of drawing it within the same batch we use for the sprites.

Just before we end the sprite batch, add the following lines:

```
auto textPos = DirectX::XMFLOAT2(10, 10);
auto textVec = DirectX::XMLoadFloat2(&textPos);
_spriteFont->DrawString(
_spriteBatch.get(),
  L"Learning Game Development",
  textVec,
  DirectX::Colors::Green
);
```

Here we need to specify the position of the text, so as before we need to get FXMVECTOR, which defines that point. To create the vector, we always have to start with XFLOAT2 or a similar type, so we'll define that as a local variable for this demonstration.

Once we have that vector, we can call `DrawString` on the sprite font. This will handle all of the drawing, and provide us with some parameters to customize the text at runtime. `SpriteFont` uses `SpriteBatch` to do rendering, so it needs a reference to that, and we need to specify the text to actually draw as a `wchar_t` string. The last mandatory parameter is the position of the text, represented by our vector from the given line.

The third parameter is one we haven't seen before, and is something that can be quite useful at runtime, even for rendering sprites. This is the `TintColor` parameter, which defines a tint to be applied to the image being drawn. Our sprite fonts are generated as pure white characters so that you can easily apply a color tint at runtime, or stick to the default white color for text.

This parameter, however, asks for a color in the form of a vector, so the `DirectX::Colors` namespace gives us access to many pre-defined common colors that you might want to use. In this case we're using green for the text, which you'll be able to see when you run the game.

If you run your game now you should see some text in the top-left corner of the screen, with the tint color you chose (green if you are following along).

Try changing the tint color or moving the text around the screen. There are plenty of things you can do with just some simple text. Change the font and take a look at the other overloads in `SpriteFont`. Rendering text can be a challenge to get right; it can break the feel of the game if it doesn't fit in. Experiment and find what fits for your visual style.

Summary

Over the course of this chapter we have learned about textures, co-ordinate systems, and fonts. We've learned some techniques that game developers use to put images and text onto the screen while maximizing performance, and we've actually gone and taken the first steps by drawing some images and writing some text to the screen.

By now you should know what DXT is and how to load these files from the disk using DirectXTK. You also know how to take these textures and draw them onto the screen with DirectXTK's `SpriteBatch`.

Don't forget that `SpriteBatch` offers a lot of benefits when you really get into drawing many things onto the screen, by batching the textures together for performance and offering sorting functionality so you can make the most of transparency.

Text rendering is a necessity for most games, and you now know how to take a font, pre-process it so you can save time at runtime, and write characters to the screen. We even covered how to apply a color tint to the text to make it more interesting.

You now know the basics of 2D rendering and are ready to apply them in making a game. There are plenty of other things you can do to make your game look awesome, so if you're interested in really pushing your 2D rendering skills, look around the many game development resources online and make some beautiful games.

Next steps

Now that we know how to get something onto the screen, we're ready to start turning this into a game. There are many more systems that contribute to the game, and the next chapter will cover some of them, with a heavy focus on getting some gameplay in there so we can take this from some static pictures to an interactive game.

3
Adding the Input

We have images on the screen, and we can see the start of a game forming, but it wouldn't be much of a game without some interactivity. The keyboard and mouse, gamepad, touch screen, or motion control — if you've played a video game then you have used one of these to tell the game what you want it to do. We need a way to play the game, and in this chapter we'll look at some of the different options that are available to get that input into the game, and add some interactivity.

Over the course of this chapter you'll learn how to add input to your game, and we'll take this further by explaining and understanding the different types of input, as well as how to use the different input devices in Windows 8.

You'll understand the following later in the chapter:

- Types of input
- The Pointer API
- Keyboard input
- XInput for the Microsoft Xbox 360 Controller

Input devices

There are four standard input devices you will encounter in your travels through the Windows game development journey. They are as follows:

- Keyboard
- Mouse
- GamePad
- Touch screen

The keyboard and mouse have traditionally been the staple of PC gaming, and continue to remain in that position for anyone with a desktop or laptop. The sheer number of options available on a keyboard combined with the precise analog input from a mouse allow for a large variety of games. Most gamers will stick to using a small selection of the available keys on the keyboard, depending on the type of game, so ensure that you consider the usability of any control scheme you create, and don't get carried away adding buttons just because the keyboard has plenty!

The mouse gives you two axes of movement information (x and y), and usually a minimum of two to three buttons. You can, of course, find mice with more than four buttons; thus, supporting a configurable control scheme is often a good idea to let the players decide if they want to use those buttons. Another thing to keep in mind is that many players may use a different keyboard configuration as compared to the common QWERTY layout. If your game supports alternate keyboard configurations then you can cater to players with any keyboard configuration, as well as those who don't like the common control configurations.

As desktops and laptops get cheaper, more and more people are shifting to use a PC as a home media center connected to their TVs. This means that they often want to play games there, and the console GamePad is one of the best ways to do this. Adding GamePad support to your game (where appropriate) is an excellent feature to easily add in, letting you reach a larger audience while making your game feel polished and complete.

In this case, the main controller that you need to add is the Xbox 360 Controller, which is supported through the XInput API that comes with the Windows 8 Software Development Kit (SDK). The controller itself provides a total of fourteen buttons, two thumbsticks, and two analog triggers. Many controllers also mimic the Xbox 360 Controller when connected to a PC, so those may be used instead. Alongside these inputs, you can even add support for the rumble motors provided in the controller, which let you provide some haptic feedback to the player by shaking the controller.

The major new addition to Windows 8 is the full support for touch-enabled devices. Tablets and touch screen laptops are becoming increasingly popular, and games on these platforms are fast becoming incredibly popular sources of entertainment. If you want to reach a massive audience, you need to ensure you have touch controls for your game. The great benefit here is that those touch controls will work on tablets, all-in-one touch PCs, and laptops with touch screens. You can expect to have at least five touch points available for use on Windows 8-certified devices.

Pointers

Touch screens are defining the current generation of devices, and to make supporting these devices easier we have a new API that combines touch, mouse, and pen input into the Pointer API. This API abstracts the type of the device away so that you can focus on the common aspect between the three different devices, the actual pointer. Unless you need built-in gestures, using the Pointer API is your best option to cover both the mouse and touch screen in one go.

The pointer events provided by Windows are exposed through the CoreWindow object that we have in our GameApplication class (this inherits from the IFrameworkView); you'll see two of them there already: OnPointerPressed and OnPointerMoved. Let's add one more to support all of the main interactions you can have using a pointer device: OnPointerReleased.

Add the following private prototype to the GameApplication.h:

```
void OnPointerReleased(Windows::UI::Core::CoreWindow^ sender,
Windows::UI::Core::PointerEventArgs^ args);
```

Now we need to connect this method up to the window event, which we will do in the SetWindow() method in the GameApplication class. The following code sets a new TypedEventHandler for pointer events, which will bind our new method to the correct event. We can bind the other two pointer events in the same way. Don't forget to implement the prototype that we've defined earlier, before continuing.

```
window->PointerReleased +=
   ref new TypedEventHandler<CoreWindow^, PointerEventArgs^>(this,
&GameApplication::OnPointerReleased);
```

In this code we want to use the pointer to let us move the player ship back and forth across the screen, by pressing the side of the screen that we want to move towards. The code isn't complex, but we need to prepare the Game class before we can hook everything up and have working touch and mouse input.

In the Game.h file, we need to add three methods and two variables. The three methods will be called by the pointer events in the GameApplication class, and the first variable will track the direction we are currently moving in, while the final variable will define the speed of the player ship.

Inside the private section of the Game class, you need to add the following:

```
int _sidePressed;
float _playerSpeed;
```

Add the following code in the public section of the Game class:

```
void PointerPressed(float x, float y);
void PointerReleased(float x, float y);
void PointerMoved(float x, float y);
```

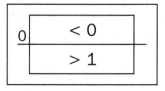

Here you can see how we will use the _sidePressed integer to define the way the player ship moves. If the player presses on the top-half of the screen, the integer will be set to -1, which will move the ship to the top of the screen, and for the bottom-half of the screen the opposite happens. This means that we can prevent the ship from moving by setting the _sidePressed to 0, as shown in the following code snippet:

```
void Game::PointerPressed(float x, float y)
{
   // Determine which side of the screen is being pressed
   _sidePressed = y - (m_windowBounds.Height / 2.0f);
}

void Game::PointerReleased(float x, float y)
{
   // Determine which side of the screen is being pressed
   _sidePressed = 0;
}

void Game::PointerMoved(float x, float y)
{
   // Determine which side of the screen is being pressed
// if we're already moving
   if (_sidePressed != 0)
     _sidePressed = y - (m_windowBounds.Height / 2.0f);
}
```

The given code determines where the pointer is being pressed, and assigns a value to _sidePressed based on the position on the screen. If the pointer is released, we need to stop moving so that the value is reset to 0.

Now that we have this code in place, we just need to move the sprite, and connect our new methods to the actual event handlers. The `Game::Update()` method is where we will be moving the sprite. As mentioned earlier, this is where the game world is updated and changed before rendering, so we can use this space (and the timing information provided) to move the sprite, as follows:

```
void Game::Update(float totalTime, float deltaTime)
{
    auto moveAmount = deltaTime * _playerSpeed;

    if (_sidePressed > 0)
    {
        _player->Y = _player->Y + moveAmount;
    }
    else if (_sidePressed < 0)
    {
        _player->Y = _player->Y - moveAmount;
    }
}
```

This method is mostly straightforward. We will take the value of `_sidePressed` and, based on whether it is less than or greater than zero, we subtract or add the right amount of movement to the Y component of the `_player` object.

The first line of the method calculates how far the sprite should be moved in this frame. If we just move each frame by a fixed amount, we would have a different experience when the frame rate fluctuated. Imagine the sprite moving 10 pixels every iteration. Now if the game runs at 30 frames per second, the sprite would move at 300 pixels per second; however, if the player has a machine that can handle the game at 60 frames per second, we will suddenly have moved double the distance in the same amount of time.

To resolve this we need the timing information generated by the `BasicTimer` class in the `GameApplication` class. Here we can retrieve the time that has passed since the previous frame as a fraction of a second, and simply multiply it by the distance to move in a second to find out our final value. This way we can specify a single value for the distance to move in a second, and be sure the sprite will move at that rate for any number of frames per second.

Now we have everything in place, and we just need to connect the `Game` class to the `GameApplication` class again before anything will work. To do this, add the following code to `OnPointerPressed`, and similar code to `OnPointerMoved` and `OnPointerReleased`.

```
void GameApplication::OnPointerPressed(CoreWindow^ sender,
PointerEventArgs^ args)
{
  auto pt = args->CurrentPoint->Position;
  m_renderer->PointerPressed(pt.X, pt.Y);
}
```

In the given code we simply extract the `Position` property from the current point provided in the arguments, and pass it directly to the respective function inside the `Game` class, which we just implemented. Now you should be able to run the game and click on (or touch) the top and bottom of the screen, and see the player sprite move towards that side. You might also want to clean up some of the content from the previous chapter if you have been following along, as we won't need the enemy sprite or text for this chapter, but leave them loading; we'll return and use those in a later chapter.

Keyboard input

We now have touch and mouse input, but many players also use desktop or laptop machines where playing with a mouse isn't the best experience. Thankfully they all have a keyboard, which will let us add some simple controls to mimic the touch controls that we currently have.

Just like the pointer system, keyboard events are raised by the `CoreWindow` object that we have in the `GameApplication` class. To begin, create some event handlers like you did for the `OnPointerReleased` handler, but use the `KeyEventArgs` instead of `PointerEventArgs`.

Add the following code in the `GameApplication.h` file:

```
void OnKeyDown(Windows::UI::Core::CoreWindow^ sender, Windows::UI::Cor
e::KeyEventArgs^ args);
void OnKeyUp(Windows::UI::Core::CoreWindow^ sender, Windows::UI::Core:
:KeyEventArgs^ args);
```

Now add the code that follows in the `GameApplication.cpp` file:

```
void GameApplication::OnKeyDown(Windows::UI::Core::CoreWindow^ sender,
Windows::UI::Core::KeyEventArgs^ args)
{
  m_renderer->KeyDown(args->VirtualKey);
}

void GameApplication::OnKeyUp(Windows::UI::Core::CoreWindow^ sender,
Windows::UI::Core::KeyEventArgs^ args)
{
  m_renderer->KeyUp(args->VirtualKey);
}
```

Here we're just passing the `VirtualKey` code through to the `KeyUp()` and `KeyDown()` methods that we need to add to the `Game` object.

Inside the `Game` class, we will define the following prototypes:

```
void KeyDown(Windows::System::VirtualKey vkey);
void KeyUp(Windows::System::VirtualKey vkey);
```

Now we can move onto the interesting part. Inside the `Game.cpp` file, we need to add the following code:

```
void Game::KeyDown(Windows::System::VirtualKey vkey)
{
  switch (vkey)
  {
  case Windows::System::VirtualKey::Left:
  case Windows::System::VirtualKey::Up:
    _sidePressed = -1;
    break;

  case Windows::System::VirtualKey::Right:
  case Windows::System::VirtualKey::Down:
    _sidePressed = 1;
    break;
  }
}

void Game::KeyUp(Windows::System::VirtualKey vkey)
{
  _sidePressed = 0;
}
```

In this code, the `KeyUp()` method is exactly the same as the `PointerReleased` handler; however, the real work is done in the `KeyDown()` method. We'll rely on the `Update()` method that we implemented earlier to handle the movement logic so `KeyDown()` can focus on changing the `_sidePressed` to trigger the right movement.

The goal of the `KeyDown()` method is to interpret the provided key code and determine if the right buttons have been clicked on, to perform a single action. For our game we want to offer the player the choice of using any of the cursor keys to control the ship, depending on what feels right for them. For that reason, we use the pass-through characteristic of case statements to allow us to perform the same action for multiple cases.

Here we're using the up and left cursor keys to move towards the top of the screen, and the down and right keys to move towards the bottom. The `Windows::System::VirtualKey` enumeration provides us with readable names for all of the available keys, making it easy to support what you need. One benefit of the `VirtualKey` is that it can be represented as an integer, making it easy to serialize for custom configurations.

There are many keys on the keyboard, and the `VirtualKey` even includes some mouse buttons and other commands to help reduce the amount of special code you need to support what are really just more buttons. The Microsoft Developer Network (MSDN) has a complete list of virtual key codes at

http://msdn.microsoft.com/en-au/library/windows/apps/windows.system.virtualkey

There's really only one input method left to cover all of the common gaming situations that Windows accommodates, and that is the GamePad.

GamePad input

Windows 8 provides native support for the Xbox 360 Controller. In most cases this will be wired; however, a wireless dongle can be acquired to allow standard wireless controllers to be used with a PC. A simple to use C API is provided that allows you to work with multiple controllers, retrieve states, and set the vibration motors on the controller so that physical feedback can be provided to the player, as required in the game.

XInput, the API for the Xbox 360 Controller, is your best option for adding GamePad support, and to get started with it we just need to include a single include file and link a static library. Inside `pch.h`, we'll add the following lines of code:

```
#include <Xinput.h>
#pragma comment(lib, "Xinput.lib")
```

Now we can get started with the controller. The Xbox 360 Controller provides a number of buttons and triggers to enable a variety of gameplay scenarios. We're just working on a simple game so we don't need to worry about all of the options. In this case we'll be supporting the vertical axis on the left thumbstick, and the up/down D-Pad buttons. They are shown in the following table:

You can find a reference for all of the buttons on the GamePad at `http://msdn.microsoft.com/en-us/library/windows/apps/microsoft.directx_sdk.reference.xinput_gamepad`

Button/Control	Description	Values
Left/right thumbstick	Analog stick(s) providing x/y axis information	-32,768 – 32,767
Left/right trigger	Analog trigger(s) positioned on the left and right sides of the controller	0 – 255
A	Green face button (right side)	Pressed/released
B	Red face button (right side)	Pressed/released
X	Blue face button (right side)	Pressed/released
Y	Yellow face button (right side)	Pressed/released
Left/right bumper	Buttons just above the triggers	Pressed/released
D-Pad	Four buttons connected to each other, pointing up, down, left, and right	Pressed/released
Back	Located in the middle of the controller, often used for going back or pausing	Pressed/released
Start	Located in the middle of the controller, often used for opening menus	Pressed/released

First of all we need to enable the XInput API, otherwise, the data retrieved from the controllers will not be meaningful. To do this, we need to add a call to the `XInputEnable()` method at the end of our `Game::LoadContent()` method. In this method we will define if we are enabling or disabling XInput using the single Boolean parameter. Once this is done, we're ready to work with the controllers.

Unlike the Pointer and Keyboard APIs, XInput requires the application to poll the API for new information. This means that for every update, we need to get the latest state of the controllers.

We could add this directly to the `Update()` method; however, the code to properly handle multiple controllers can get a little too long for that single method, so let's break that out into a dedicated GamePad update method and call it from the start of the `Update()` method.

The following is the complete `UpdateGamePad()` method. Don't worry about the length, we'll break it down.

```cpp
void Game::UpdateGamePad()
{
  DWORD result;
  XINPUT_STATE state;
  for (DWORD i = 0; i < XUSER_MAX_COUNT; ++i)
  {
    ZeroMemory(&state, sizeof(XINPUT_STATE));
    result = XInputGetState(i, &state);
    if (result == ERROR_SUCCESS)
    {
      auto btnState = state.Gamepad.wButtons;
      if (btnState & XINPUT_GAMEPAD_DPAD_UP)
      {
        _sidePressed = -1;
      }
      else if (btnState & XINPUT_GAMEPAD_DPAD_DOWN)
      {
        _sidePressed = 1;
      }
      else
      {
        float thumbY = state.Gamepad.sThumbLY;
        float magnitude = abs(thumbY);
        if (magnitude > XINPUT_GAMEPAD_LEFT_THUMB_DEADZONE)
        {
          if (thumbY > 0)
            _sidePressed = -1;
          else
            _sidePressed = 1;
        }
        else
        {
          _sidePressed = 0;
        }
      }
    }
  }
}
```

Multiple controllers

Upto four controllers can be connected to one machine, as indicated by the XUSER_MAX_COUNT constant provided by XInput. We can work with all of the controllers by looping through all of them and retrieving their state using the XInputGetState() method. This method takes the integer index of the controller we want, and a pointer to an XINPUT_STATE structure that will contain the state of the controller.

The player may not always have four controllers plugged in, though, so we want to be able to support a controller on any index if it's plugged in. The XInputGetState() method provides us with an error or success message depending on whether the state could be acquired, and with that we can determine if we're looking at a connected controller based on whether the result is equal to ERROR_SUCCESS, as shown:

```
DWORD result;
XINPUT_STATE state;
for (DWORD i = 0; i < XUSER_MAX_COUNT; ++i)
{
  ZeroMemory(&state, sizeof(XINPUT_STATE));
  result = XInputGetState(i, &state);
  if (result == ERROR_SUCCESS)
```

Buttons

One of the main components of a GamePad are the buttons. Using XInput these are pretty simple to work with, and are shown in the code snippet that follows:

```
auto btnState = state.Gamepad.wButtons;
if (btnState & XINPUT_GAMEPAD_DPAD_UP)
{
  _sidePressed = -1;
}
else if (btnState & XINPUT_GAMEPAD_DPAD_DOWN)
{
  _sidePressed = 1;
}
```

The buttons are stored inside the Gamepad object, packed into a single word, meaning that we need to make use of the AND bitwise operation to check if the button has been pressed. We can make use of some predefined constants to extract the correct buttons, as outlined in the following table:

Button	#define
D-Pad up	XINPUT_GAMEPAD_DPAD_UP
D-Pad down	XINPUT_GAMEPAD_DPAD_DOWN
D-Pad left	XINPUT_GAMEPAD_DPAD_LEFT
D-Pad right	XINPUT_GAMEPAD_DPAD_RIGHT
A	XINPUT_GAMEPAD_A
B	XINPUT_GAMEPAD_B
X	XINPUT_GAMEPAD_X
Y	XINPUT_GAMEPAD_Y

For a full list of the buttons, visit http://msdn.microsoft.com/en-us/library/windows/apps/microsoft.directx_sdk.reference.xinput_gamepad

Deadzones and thumbsticks

We have buttons! Specifically the D-Pad for moving the ship around. But that isn't the usual movement control for games that use the Xbox 360 Controller. Alongside our existing options we need to add support for the thumbstick, which is the common form of input for character and camera movement. In particular we want to add in support for the left thumbstick, which is the player movement control. This is done as follows:

```
float thumbY = state.Gamepad.sThumbLY;
float magnitude = abs(thumbY);
if (magnitude > XINPUT_GAMEPAD_LEFT_THUMB_DEADZONE)
{
  if (thumbY > 0)
    _sidePressed = -1;
  else
    _sidePressed = 1;
}
else
{
  _sidePressed = 0;
}
```

To do this, we can extract the vertical (y axis) value from the state object using the sThumbLY field. If you want to get the X component from the right thumbstick, you should use the sThumbRX field. You can determine which stick and axis you're retrieving from the name.

This field gives us a SHORT object that defines the location of the stick, with the positive values pointing up, and the negative values pointing down. This is, however, an analog device and the value you get when the stick isn't being touched is often non-zero. This is where the deadzone comes into play. The deadzone is a threshold within which all input is ignored. This allows the players to rest their thumbs on the stick and not worry about the game reacting to the tiny movements that are created. XInput provides standard values for the deadzone on each thumbstick, so it's recommended that you make use of those defined constants for a good experience.

To calculate if the thumbstick is sitting within the deadzone, we get the absolute value of the y axis and check if this value is greater than the threshold. If we don't get the absolute value first, we'll end up ignoring any negative values, which represents the entire down direction. Once we've filtered out values within the deadzone we can use the original value to determine if the player is moving up or down, and set the _sidePressed variable appropriately.

Now you can test this with a connected controller if you have one, and you should be able to use either the D-Pad or left thumbstick to move the player sprite up and down the screen, just like you can with a mouse, keyboard, or touch screen.

Summary

In this chapter you have implemented basic input for the game, and moved the player ship up and down the screen. As you can see, there are many different input devices available for Windows, and supporting the core three is easy with the XInput API and built-in Pointer/Keyboard APIs. XInput adds support for many other peripherals from racing wheels to dance pads. Consider what devices are best for your game, but remember that, for Windows, most people will play on a tablet or traditional machine, so having support for touch screens and keyboard/mouse is crucial, with GamePads as a great addition on the side.

Next steps

Now that we have input and drawing, we're ready to add in the main gameplay for the game. In the next chapter we'll look at the different subsystems such as Artificial Intelligence and Physics that are used to make the game simulation feel real. We'll also look at the ways of structuring the internals of the game, using an entity system to represent the different objects, and how they tie together. In the next chapter we will have a game, with all of the logic in place, ready to be played and extended.

4
Adding the Play in the Gameplay

Now that we have our input in place, we're ready to add it in the gameplay and turn this collection of systems into a game. There are many different systems that work together to make the game interactive and playable. Not all of these are needed for all games, however, so you need to look at what your game requires and only implement what is needed.

In this chapter you will learn about the different software modules involved in making a game, and see how to implement them into the sample game that you are creating. We want to create a game where the players control their space ships, destroying enemies that fly toward them with basic Artificial Intelligence (the logic that allows the computer to appear intelligent and make decisions, often autonomously). To achieve this, we need to look at ways of structuring a game, how to manage the different objects on screen, and how to communicate between the different systems to make everything work. Right now we have input and graphics; however, we need to still make some changes to make these easier to work with. We'll begin by implementing a system to manage the ships and objects in the game, and then adjust the existing systems to work nicely.

While working on this game, we will cover the following topics:

- Structuring our gameplay objects
- Collision detection
- Improving the renderer
- Spawning enemies
- Add some AI to the enemies
- Victory and defeat states

Structuring a game

One of the first things you need to remember when working with game development is that there are many ways to structure games, and each has its own benefits and problems. Designing the right architecture for your game can lead to many benefits, and just as when creating any other application you should consider your options and how well they fit the type of game you are creating. Let's take a look at some widely-used options.

Traditional object-oriented design

One way to design games is to use the traditional object-oriented approach. Here we treat the different parts of the game as objects that represent what they represent in the game. For example, a ship in the game would consist of a Ship class, or a bullet in the game would consist of a Bullet class. By utilizing inheritance, different types of Ship objects can be provided, and a common code can be reused by each type, reducing the workload required to develop the functionality.

Let's take a look at how we would structure this game using this method. First let's identify the visible objects we have that affect the gameplay:

- Player
- Enemies
- Bullets
- Bombs
- Power ups
- Score
- Background

There are some other objects that we need to consider alongside the ones mentioned in the preceding list:

- AI Paths
- Transforms (X/Y/Rotation)
- Settings
- Screens (Main menu/In-game)
- Enemy Spawner(s)
- Input Manager

- Enemy Manager
- Bullet Manager
- Renderer
- Texture

The main issue with this style of design is that the code you write will be focused on the type of game being made. If you want to re-use the code later on, it will be harder to do this without extensive changes to the existing code. Code re-use with OOP may be difficult even within the context of the current game, where certain types may share the functionality, but cannot be easily structured to share that code. Of course in many cases this is not a problem and using this style of design allows for faster development.

As an example, let's look at the logic flow involved in shooting an enemy in this game. The player begins by triggering the input for shooting, which is detected by the input manager. Code handling the input would then call `player->Shoot()` and that object would create a new bullet, which moves forward for each update — perhaps with a `Move()` method. When the bullet reaches the enemy it detects the collision, destroys itself, and calls `enemy->Damage(damage)`, passing the amount of damage the bullet should do to the enemy so that it can appropriately reduce its health. The enemy then checks the amount of health remaining and if it is zero (or less than zero) it destroys itself.

When a bullet or enemy destroys itself, it is removed from the respective manager and renderer so that it is not displayed or used anymore.

Components and entities

Another design style uses **composition** to disconnect the objects from each other, making it easier to construct them as required, and add/remove functionality as needed. This also improves re-using in future games because the components can be taken and easily copied over, knowing that they have very low coupling to other objects. This, however, requires a bit of design to build the systems and provide helpers or systems to allow communication between them.

The core of this system uses the concept of an **entity** (sometimes called an **actor**) to represent all of the objects in the game. The entity is often a bare bones simple class that contains the necessary functionality to store components and allow for discovery or generic communication paths between the components.

The components themselves define what an entity is, and are often also managed by separate manager classes that handle updating or iterating through them in sequence. This has a number of benefits, ranging from high modularity to performance. This is also one of the first steps to a concept called **data-oriented design** (not to be confused with data-driven design) that looks at how memory is used and structured to make parallelism much easier while providing performance benefits by using the CPU cache in a smarter way.

Note that some objects are still represented by classes and are not appropriate for the **entity/component system**. Things such as screens and settings are usually specific or sit above this system, and so you would still treat them as you would with object-oriented design.

If we were to look at the classes defined in the previous design style, we can come up with the following components:

- Transform
- Health
- Weapon
- Score
- AI/Path (Enemy Controller)
- Input Action
- Texture
- Power-up (Loot/pick-up functionality)
- Enemy Spawner
- Bullet Controller
- Collision Shape

These components may be managed by themselves, or grouped together to make processing easier. By batching component updates together, you can also make better use of the CPU data cache, which can help to improve performance.

You have a choice when creating interaction between different components. You can have them search for the other components and then directly call them, or you can implement a messaging system through the entity that allows you to remove all dependencies between the components. Better yet, consider using both methods and use them where appropriate (for example, use messaging for independent components, and direct communication for components that need to know about each other).

Let's take a look at the same scenario as before, but with this system in place. To begin with we still have an Input Manager that will detect input from the user; it then passes control to the Input Action, which connects the logic to the button. The Input Action is a component connected to the player entity, so that when it fires, the action communicates with the Bullet Manager to create a new bullet entity. Inside this entity is a Bullet Controller, which acts as the brains for the bullet. The bullet manager can then loop through the Bullet Controllers during an update, which allows them to move the bullet forward. Once the collision system detects a collision between the bullet collision shapes, the controller can detect this state and destroy the bullet entity. The enemy has its own controller, a collision shape, and a health component. The Bullet Controller determines the enemy entity from the collision and notifies its Health Component that it should take damage using the appropriate value. The Health Component then determines if the enemy is still alive. The Enemy Controller can then detect the health and destroy the enemy. Alternatively the Health Component can check its state and destroy the enemy itself if desired.

There are many different ways you can assign control and responsibility, so that you have the flexibility to choose what is best for your game. If only the enemies have health, you could add that as a field to the enemy controller and remove the health component. However if you keep the health controller, it's quite easy to add in support for enemies that shoot the player, by just adding in code to tell the enemies to shoot, and creating a health object for the player.

Putting it all together

Let's put together some classes that will support the mechanics in our game, and then build on these later in the chapter to complete them. But before we write any code, be sure to clean out all of the test code we wrote into Game.h and Game.cpp. We'll be taking those visuals and turning them into a set of objects that should make designing the logic easier.

 To make things simpler, and not jump between native C++ and C++/CX all the time, we will change the texture from a reference class to a native class.

To begin, we need two classes: one which we will call Ship, and the other Player.

The code for `Ship.h` is as follows:

```
typedef enum
{
    Up,
    Down,
    Left,
    Right
} ShipDirection;

class Ship abstract
{
protected:
  XMFLOAT2 _position;
  float _rotation;
  XMFLOAT2 _scale;

  std::shared_ptr<Sprite> _sprite;
  void LoadTexture(std::wstring &path);

  int _health;
  float _speed;

  bool _isAlive;

public:
  Ship(void);
  ~Ship(void);

  void Move(ShipDirection direction, float deltaTime);
  void MoveTo(float x, float y);

  void Damage(int amount);
  bool GetIsAlive();
  void SetIsAlive(bool value);
  void Reset();

  DirectX::XMFLOAT2 GetTextureSize();
};
```

The code for `Player.h` is as follows:

```
class Player :
  public Ship
{
public:
  Player(void);
```

```
~Player(void);

void Load();

void BindInput(float screenHeight);
void Update(float deltaTime);
};
```

Here you can see the class definitions for both. The ship will serve as our common base class for both the `Player` and the `Enemy`. It will contain some basic information such as the position and rotation, as well as (in future) the texture of the ship. Alongside that we also have the health of the ship, which will be monitored by the base class.

Inside the `Ship` class, we have some helper methods to handle loading the sprite and managing the lifetime of the object, which we will put to use later on. We won't define the visual code for the `Ship` yet as we will handle that when we get to the rendering system later on.

Inside our `Game` class, let's start by adding a pointer to a Player object, and new that up inside `LoadContent`. At the same time let's call `player->Load()` and `BindInput` as follows.

```
_player = new Player();
_player->BindInput(m_renderTargetSize.Height);
_player->Load();
```

This will trigger our methods to set up the graphics and input code that we will add in later on when we reach those respective systems.

We added a `Ship` base class for a reason. Even though they oppose each other, the player and the enemies are both common in many ways. Why repeat code when the only real difference is the logic behind the control of each ship?

Add in an `Enemy` class and give it the following definition:

```
class Enemy :
  public Ship
{
public:
  Enemy(void);
  ~Enemy(void);

  void Load();
  void Update(float deltaTime);
};
```

You can see this is pretty similar to the `Player` class but, as we don't need to control the enemy, we don't need a method to set up the input system. Now let's take a look at the implementation of the `Load` method for both of these objects. Here we'll use the `LoadTexture` helper defined in `Ship` to load in the right texture for each type of object. For the player, we want to add the following call:

```
void Player::Load()
{
  LoadTexture(std::wstring(L"textures\\player.DDS"));
  _sprite->Rotation = XM_PIDIV2;
  auto texSize = _sprite->GetSize();
  MoveTo(
    _position.x + (texSize.x / 2.0f),
    _position.y + (texSize.y / 2.0f));
}
```

In the preceding code we load the player as well as set its position using the `MoveTo` helper that we will define later. In this case we're just adjusting the object so that it is completely on the screen by accessing the size of the texture and then shifting the position so it sits in the middle of the texture.

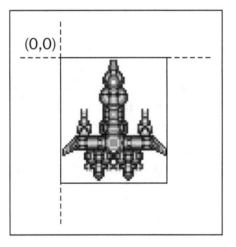

We will define the **origin** of the texture later on, and this will define the point around which the texture rotates, as well as the offset for the texture when placed in the world. Normally the texture would have an origin of `0,0`, which would be at the top-left corner as shown in the preceding figure; however, we want to place the origin in the centre so that the texture rotates correctly.

For the enemy we want the following:

```
void Enemy::Load()
{
  LoadTexture(std::wstring(L"textures\\enemy.DDS"));
  _sprite->Rotation = -XM_PIDIV2;
}
```

This is much simpler, but we will be specifying the position of the enemy at a later point, so we don't need to worry about that for now.

Also note the rotation lines for both the `Player` and `Enemy`. If you take a look at the provided art assets you'll see that both ships point upwards and, if rendered without change, you'll have both ships pointing up instead of towards each other as they should. Here we're just telling the sprite that it needs to be rotated by 90 degrees and -90 degrees for the player and enemy, respectively. We do this by using the **radian** representation of the angle, which you'll find is common in game development. For reference, the conversion between radians and degrees can be done with the following formulae:

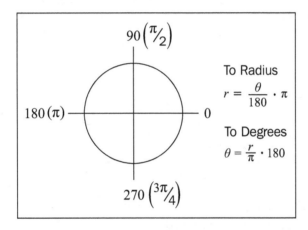

In a lot of cases just remembering that 180 degrees is equal to π radians will be enough, as it is here, where to get 90 degrees we can just say π/2 radians, which is the equivalent of 180/2 degrees.

We'll leave the `Player->BindInput` method alone for now because that will require the addition of input code, and instead look at the enemy movement. In this game the enemies will be moving from right to left at a constant rate of speed. If you look back at the `Ship` definition, we have a helper method called `Move`, which allows us to specify a direction and the time since the last frame. This method when implemented will use the `_speed` property of the `Ship` to move the object in the specified direction, relative to the amount of time since we last updated. Pretty simple! So let's implement the code to do this movement. Change to `Ship.cpp` and implement `Ship::Move`, as shown in the following code:

```
void Ship::Move(ShipDirection direction, float deltaTime)
{
  auto amount = deltaTime * _speed;
  switch (direction)
  {
  case ShipDirection::Up:
    _position.y -= amount;
    break;

  case ShipDirection::Down:
    _position.y += amount;
    break;

  case ShipDirection::Left:
    _position.x -= amount;
    break;

  case ShipDirection::Right:
    _position.x += amount;
    break;
  };
  if (_sprite != nullptr)
    _sprite->Position = _position;
}
```

No matter what direction the ship is moving in, it will always move a certain amount in the frame, so we can calculate that up front by simply multiplying the speed with the time since last frame (`deltaTime`). Now we just use a switch statement to add that amount to the position based on the chosen direction. For `ShipDirection::Left` and `ShipDirection::Right`, we need to subtract and add, respectively, and for `Up`/`Down` we need to do the same thing: subtract and add. After that we need to ensure this new position propagates to the `Sprite` object so that when we get around to drawing the texture, it will show up in the right place.

While we're here, let's take a look at the rest of the methods inside `Ship`.

```
void Ship::MoveTo(float x, float y)
{
  _position.x = x;
  _position.y = y;
  _sprite->Position = _position;
}

void Ship::Damage(int amount)
{
  _health -= amount;
  if (_health <= 0)
    SetIsAlive(false);
}

bool Ship::GetIsAlive()
{
  return _isAlive;
}

void Ship::SetIsAlive(bool value)
{
  _isAlive = value;
  _sprite->Visible = value;
}

void Ship::Reset()
{
  _health = Health;
  SetIsAlive(true);
}
```

Starting from the top, `MoveTo` allows us to specify an absolute position and jump the ship there, including the `Sprite`. This will be useful when we spawn the enemies, as we need to position them in the right place.

`Damage`, `GetIsAlive`, `SetIsAlive`, and `Reset` all manage the health status of the ship and allow for other objects to damage the ship and eventually destroy it.

So we have the enemies and player well defined, but this new `Enemy` class isn't actually in use yet. Return to the `Game` class and add the following private variables:

```
std::vector<Enemy*> _enemies;
float _sinceLastSpawn;
```

Once those are in, we need to add the following to `LoadContent`:

```
for (auto i = 0; i < MaxEnemies; ++i)
{
  auto e = new Enemy();
  e->Load();
  e->SetIsAlive(false);
  _enemies.push_back(e);
}
```

This lets us create a **pool** of enemies that we can spawn in the game-based on a spawn timer. A pool is a pre-defined collection that allows us to re-use objects. This has the benefit of removing constant allocations and de-allocations, which is often slow. We can adjust some of the values, such as the total number of enemies based on our needs, but for now let's just fix that at 5, which we can do with a simple constant in `Game.cpp`.

The spawning itself happens inside the `Update` method within `Game`, shown as follows:

```
_sinceLastSpawn += deltaTime;
int numAlive = 0;
for (auto enemy : _enemies)
{
  if (enemy->GetIsAlive())
  {
    enemy->Update(deltaTime);
    numAlive++;
  }
}

if (_sinceLastSpawn >= SpawnTime)
{
  _sinceLastSpawn -= SpawnTime;
  if (numAlive < MaxEnemies)
  {
    for (auto enemy : _enemies)
    {
      if (!enemy->GetIsAlive())
      {
        auto texSize = enemy->GetTextureSize();
        auto y = texSize.y +
          ((float)rand() / (float)RAND_MAX) *
          (m_renderTargetSize.Height - (texSize.y * 2));
        enemy->MoveTo(m_renderTargetSize.Width, y);
```

```
        enemy->Reset();
        break;
      }
    }
  }
}
```

Here we begin with just a standard update loop for the enemy. However, we don't bother to update the enemy if it isn't alive. As this game won't have thousands of enemies we don't need to worry about writing a different system to avoid extra iterations. Now we move onto the spawning part of the code, where the real work is done.

In here we only want to spawn if there has been enough time since the last spawn. We track this using _sinceLastSpawn, which is updated with the deltaTime value each update.

Once it exceeds the limit, which is just a constant defined with a value of 5, we can jump the value back to start counting again and then move on with spawning. In the next if statement we're just checking if the number of enemies currently alive is within the limit of our pool of enemies so we don't try and add in enemies that haven't been created.

After that we find the first dead enemy and spawn it past the right side of the screen (X = ScreenWidth) with a random Y value. We finish up by resetting the enemy to ensure it is flagged as Alive and has full health.

So now we have much of the game logic in place. For the rest we need to establish some sub-systems to manage tasks such as Input, Rendering, and Collision, which will let us add in the final pieces of the puzzle.

Subsystems

How we structure our game state plays a large role in deciding how the engine is structured; however, the structure of the subsystems that run all of the logic of the game is also important.

There are three subsystems that are usually required for all games:

- Rendering
- Audio
- Input

Of course some of these are still optional depending on what your game requires, so add and remove as needed. For the game we are making we will make use of rendering and input to get interaction in place.

Now let's take a look at some of the decisions that need to be made when designing these systems. The first revolves around access and **visibility**. These systems need to be accessible from many locations in the game and, depending on how you structure your game state, you may be able to restrict this, or you may be making it harder for yourself in the end. A common pattern used in games for these systems is the **singleton** pattern. If you haven't encountered this before, the singleton pattern describes a way to create classes that are accessible through global scope while ensuring that only one instance exists. We also gain control over the creation and destruction of the instance, which is important to ensure we use resources appropriately and initialize in the correct order. This has downsides, of course. The global scope means that you can now easily access the instance from anywhere, but in doing so it's easy to increase your coupling and reduce the quality of the code. With a little effort you can work to ensure that you pass the references required to all parts of your game that need the references. You need to balance the trade-offs and decide if you can live with the code issues that may arise in the future; however, many games can live with that as games tend to not require a lot of module reuse. For the purposes of this book we will use the singleton pattern so that we can focus on the game code and not waste time.

Now let's take a look at some of the core systems required in a bit more detail, and determine how we will structure these systems for the sample game.

Refining the input system

One of the first things processed during an update, and one of the most important systems for interactivity, is the input system. We need a system that allows for multiple forms of input, from keyboard and mouse to touch and gamepad. But alongside that we need to be able to extend it to the future chapters when we add in support for sensors.

Another thing we need to consider is if we want to let the user change the controls and, if so, whether we want to restrict that to a selection of presets or allow them to completely reconfigure the control set. The more freedom you provide, the more effort on your part; however, players will thank you for the option. What you choose here can also depend on the system you are developing for. If you are just working with a touch screen you generally don't need to provide configurable input as there isn't much to change; however, the more buttons that you provide the more players will want to change their input.

For our game we're going to use an action based input system. Using this system we define actions that link to the logic of the game, for example, MoveLeft. By Connecting to these actions are triggers, which define the different ways our input devices can trigger the action.

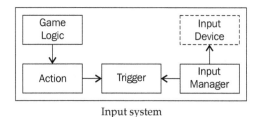

Input system

To understand how this all works together, let's look at the action of moving our ship to the left. We have three different input systems for the game at the moment:

- Keyboard
- Touch
- GamePad

Certain actions on each of these input devices will all map to the same action: moving the player ship to the left. In our game the player could use any of these input devices, so we need to be able to support them all.

First the system will check for input using all of the triggers. The input manager retrieves states from all of the input devices and then iterates through the triggers, checking if any of the device states satisfy the triggers. If so, the associated action is marked as triggered, ready for the game play logic to act on later. At some point all of the actions are also cleared (usually at the beginning of the input update) to clean the input state for a new update.

So now let's implement this system. First we'll define three classes, Trigger, Action, and InputManager, which will work together to build the aforementioned system.

Trigger

This is just a simple base class for the triggers we will define for different input types:

```
class Trigger
{
public:
  virtual bool IsTriggered(InputManager *input) = 0;
};
```

We'll look at how triggers work when we define one later.

Action

`Action` has some helpers to create and store Triggers as well as provide a way for the `InputManager` to quickly update the state of the input system.

```
class Action
{
private:
  std::vector<Trigger*> _triggers;
  bool _isTriggered;

public:
  bool enabled;

  Action();
  ~Action();

  template <class T>
  T* CreateTrigger()
  {
    auto t = new T();
    _triggers.push_back(t);
    return t;
  };

  void Update(InputManager *input);

  bool IsTriggered() { return _isTriggered; }
};
```

The update method is pretty straightforward. It loops through the triggers linked to it until it finds the first one to trigger, at which point it sets its own _isTriggered flag to signal to the code watching the action that the user has done whatever input is necessary.

```
void Action::Update(InputManager *input)
{
  _isTriggered = false;
  for (auto trigger : _triggers)
  {
    _isTriggered = trigger->IsTriggered(input);
    if (_isTriggered)
      break;
  }
}
```

InputManager

This is a lot to work on, but once implemented you'll have a pretty useful input system that with only minor extensions could be used in other games.

```cpp
typedef enum
{
  Released,
  Pressed,
  JustReleased
} KeyState;

class InputManager
{
private:
  static InputManager *_inst;
  InputManager();
  ~InputManager();

  std::vector<Action*> _actions;

  bool _keyStatus[166]; // There are 166 VirtualKeys
  bool _pointerDown;
  float _pointerX;
  float _pointerY;
  XINPUT_STATE _padState[XUSER_MAX_COUNT];

  void UpdateGamePad();

public:
  static InputManager* GetInstance();
  static void DestroyInstance();

  Action* CreateAction();

  void Update();

  void TrackKeyDown(Windows::System::VirtualKey key);
  void TrackKeyUp(Windows::System::VirtualKey key);
  void TrackPointerPressed(float x, float y);
  void TrackPointerReleased(float x, float y);
  void TrackPointerMoved(float x, float y);

  bool IsKeyDown(Windows::System::VirtualKey key);
  bool IsPointerPressed();
  void GetPointerPos(float *x, float *y);

  XINPUT_STATE GetGamepadState(int userIndex);
};
```

The `InputManager` stores the actions that have been created, as well as the state of the input devices that are gathered not only during the update loop, but also from events sent by the main application.

`KeyState` is an enumeration that we will use later to allow us to trigger based on if the key (or pointer) was pressed, released, or "just released," which refers to the frame right after the input switches from pressed to released.

Within the public methods we have methods to manage the singleton aspect of this manager, allowing access from anywhere while ensuring we are just talking to one `InputManager`. Alongside that are all of the methods required to update the input devices, including ways to pass through the key and pointer events that we saw in the last chapter.

For the implementation of `InputManager`, I'll leave it as an exercise to the reader to implement the singleton and input device functionality. Refer to the previous chapter or the sample code for a reference implementation.

```
void InputManager::Update()
{
  UpdateGamePad();
  for (auto action : _actions)
  {
    if (action->enabled)
      action->Update(this);
  }
}
```

The `Update` method in the `InputManager` defines the start of the input processing, and begins by updating the GamePad, which is not an event based system. From there it processes all of the enabled actions to update the state of the input system.

`UpdateGamePad` simply runs a cut down version of the gamepad state code in *Chapter 3, Adding the Input*. Here we store state for each of the connected gamepads and don't do any other processing, instead leaving that to the trigger and the game code.

With all of this together we just need to define triggers, which provide the code to check if an input has triggered, and we will be able to use the input system for our player object.

Triggers

The triggers allow us to customize different input systems and styles based on the raw input data. This way we could define gestures for touch input or multiple button presses to trigger a single action. We'll start simple and just work with a single key-press trigger, which will be called `KeyTrigger`:

```
class KeyTrigger :
  public Trigger
{
private:
  Windows::System::VirtualKey _key;
  KeyState _state;
  KeyState _expectedState;

public:
  KeyTrigger() : _key(Windows::System::VirtualKey::None), _expectedSta
te(KeyState::Released) {};

  virtual bool IsTriggered(InputManager *input);
  void SetData(Windows::System::VirtualKey key, KeyState state);
};
```

This class just uses the standard windows `VirtualKey` enumeration to define the desired key, and the `KeyState` enumeration we defined earlier to indicate when to trigger. In the public block of methods we just define some defaults and implement the pure virtual method defined in the abstract `Trigger` base class. Alongside that we provide a method to set the expected key and when to trigger so that we can configure this object as required.

For this class, `IsTriggered` is pretty simple and looks like the following.

```
bool KeyTrigger::IsTriggered(InputManager *input)
{
  if (input->IsKeyDown(_key))
    _state = KeyState::Pressed;
  else if (_state == KeyState::Pressed)
    _state = KeyState::JustReleased;
  else
    _state = KeyState::Released;

  return _state == _expectedState;
}
```

This is just a simple example of checking the state of the key against the state provided by `InputManager`, and then adjusting the state accordingly so we can get a Boolean value indicating if the state matches the expected state set using `SetData`.

To handle the GamePad we need to define an enumeration that outlines the available buttons.

```
typedef enum
{
  None = 0,
  DPad_Up = XINPUT_GAMEPAD_DPAD_UP,
  DPad_Down = XINPUT_GAMEPAD_DPAD_DOWN,
  DPad_Left = XINPUT_GAMEPAD_DPAD_LEFT,
  DPad_Right = XINPUT_GAMEPAD_DPAD_RIGHT,
  Start = XINPUT_GAMEPAD_START,
  Back = XINPUT_GAMEPAD_BACK,
  LeftThumbStick = XINPUT_GAMEPAD_LEFT_THUMB,
  RightThumbStick = XINPUT_GAMEPAD_RIGHT_THUMB,
  LeftShoulder = XINPUT_GAMEPAD_LEFT_SHOULDER,
  RightShoulder = XINPUT_GAMEPAD_RIGHT_SHOULDER,
  A = XINPUT_GAMEPAD_A,
  B = XINPUT_GAMEPAD_B,
  X = XINPUT_GAMEPAD_X,
  Y = XINPUT_GAMEPAD_Y
} GamepadButtons;
```

We can then use this in a fashion similar to KeyTrigger by replacing `VirtualKey` with `GamepadButtons` inside our new `GamepadButtonTrigger` class.

```
class GamepadButtonTrigger :
  public Trigger
{
private:
  GamepadButtons _button;
  KeyState _state;
  KeyState _expectedState;

public:
  GamepadButtonTrigger() : _button(GamepadButtons::None), _expectedSta
te(KeyState::Released) {};

  virtual bool IsTriggered(InputManager *input);
  void SetData(GamepadButtons button, KeyState state);
};
```

The code for this is almost the same as `KeyTrigger`; however, to retrieve the state of the button from `InputManager` we need to get the `wButtons` word and bitwise-and it against the expected button to get a Boolean. For more information on this please refer back to *Chapter 3, Adding the Input*.

```
auto xState = input->GetGamepadState(0);
auto isSet = (xState.Gamepad.wButtons & (WORD)_button) > 0;
```

The final trigger we will define is `PointerAxisBoundsTrigger`. This one is a bit of a mouthful but it essentially lets us define a region of the screen that fires the trigger if the player presses within.

We'll begin by specifying a new type that provides the `Lower` and `Upper` bounds for a single axis. We'll use this in the game code to allow the player to press anywhere within the top or bottom half of the screen and move the ship towards that side.

```
typedef struct
{
    float Lower;
    float Upper;
} AxisBounds;

AxisBounds CreateAxisBounds(float lower, float upper);
```

Here we can also define a helper method to make it a little easier to create the `AxisBounds` structure.

```
class PointerAxisBoundsTrigger :
    public Trigger
{
private:
    bool _hasX, _hasY;
    AxisBounds _x, _y;
    KeyState _state, _expectedState;

    bool IsWithinBounds(AxisBounds& b, float pt);

public:
    virtual bool IsTriggered(InputManager *input);
    void SetData(AxisBounds *xBounds, AxisBounds *yBounds, KeyState
expectedState);
};
```

This block of code defines the class, and you can see it is similar but it has an extra helper to allow us to separate out the code checking if a provided pointer's point is within the bounds.

```
bool PointerAxisBoundsTrigger::IsWithinBounds(AxisBounds& b, float pt)
{
  return (pt > b.Lower) && (pt < b.Upper);
}
```

`IsWithinBounds` is a pretty simple method that just does a basic check to see if the point is between the lower and upper values.

```
bool PointerAxisBoundsTrigger::IsTriggered(InputManager *input)
{
  float ptrX, ptrY;
  input->GetPointerPos(&ptrX, &ptrY);
  bool result = _hasX || _hasY;

  if (_hasX)
    result &= IsWithinBounds(_x, ptrX);

  if (_hasY)
    result &= IsWithinBounds(_y, ptrY);

  auto pressed = input->IsPointerPressed();
  if (pressed)
    _state = KeyState::Pressed;
  else if (_state == KeyState::Pressed)
    _state = KeyState::JustReleased;
  else
    _state = KeyState::Released;

  return result && (_state == _expectedState);
}
```

`IsTriggered` is where most of the work is done, and most of this is new except for the bit at the end that you will recognize. We begin by retrieving the pointer position from `InputManager`, and then determine if bounds have been set for either axis. We can then test the point against each set axis to determine if it is within one or both, and from there determine if the pointer is pressed so we can check against the expected state.

With this trigger we now have all of the required code to implement keyboard, touch, and GamePad-based inputs for the game.

As an exercise, how would you implement a trigger to check for input on the GamePad thumbsticks?

Now that we have all of this, let's put it to use by adding in the input control for the player. Begin by defining two actions within `Player.h`:

```
Action *_actionMoveUp;
Action *_actionMoveDown;
```

Now we can move to the `BindInput` method in `Player.cpp` to build up these actions using the triggers we created.

 This code is missing some parts for size. Just implement the full set of triggers based on the pattern provided. A reference implementation can be found in the sample code for this chapter (`Player.cpp`).

```
auto im = InputManager::GetInstance();
auto halfScreen = screenHeight / 2.0f;
AxisBounds downBounds = CreateAxisBounds(halfScreen, screenHeight);
AxisBounds upBounds = CreateAxisBounds(0, halfScreen);
```

We start by getting a reference to the `InputManager`, and then determining the size of the screen so that we can specify the bounds for the Y axis.

```
_actionMoveDown = im->CreateAction();
auto downPtrTrigger = _actionMoveDown->CreateTrigger<PointerAxisBound
sTrigger>();
downPtrTrigger->SetData(nullptr, &downBounds, KeyState::Pressed);

// ...

_actionMoveUp = im->CreateAction();
auto upPadTrigger = _actionMoveUp->CreateTrigger<GamepadButtonTrigg
er>();
upPadTrigger->SetData(GamepadButtons::DPad_Up, KeyState::Pressed);
```

Once we have created the actions with `InputManager`, it's just two lines to create a new trigger based on the type we want and set the desired data. In the first example, we use `AxisBounds` created earlier to define a `PointerAxisBoundsTrigger`, for which we just define the Y axis, passing `nullptr` to the X axis.

For the second action we have example code for setting a `GamepadButtonTrigger`, which is very similar to the `KeyTrigger`, as you just saw.

We can now fill out the `Update` method:

```cpp
void Player::Update(float deltaTime)
{
  if (_actionMoveDown->IsTriggered())
  {
    Move(ShipDirection::Down, deltaTime);
  }
  else if(_actionMoveUp->IsTriggered())
  {
    Move(ShipDirection::Up, deltaTime);
  }
}
```

Based on the state of each action we simply call the `Move` helper command to move up or down as required. Of course don't forget to hook up the `InputManager` to each of the `Key` and `Pointer` events in `Game.cpp`.

With all of this in place you should now be able to move the player ship around. Of course you can't see it yet because we need to write in a way to render the system, using a renderer to manage everything.

Renderer

The renderer is just an encapsulation of the texture loading and drawing code we have created so far. We will use the renderer to keep track of a scene, which refers to all of the visual objects in the game world, and draw everything in the scene. At the same time the renderer can provide a number of other features that can be useful to complex games.

Resource management

Content gets re-used in games quite a bit, and if you had to load each texture and piece of data for every instance you would waste a lot of memory. To get around this we need some form of resource management. As usual for games there are many ways to go about implementing this, from a really simple cache to a complex memory and resource manager that sits separate to all other sub-systems in the game. For our sample we'll add a really simple resource manager to the renderer to cache the textures as they are loaded, but for a larger game this is insufficient, so let's take a look at what usually goes into the design of a resource manager.

To get started, we need to have a way to work with the filesystem. Some games store resources as individual files on the disk; however, this creates a lot of overhead seeking between the different files. To get around this many games implement a packaging system that combines the files together to allow for faster loads by reading from a block of disk space rather than random files. This has the benefit in some situations of allowing the package to be loaded into memory as a block of data and then the resources are extracted from there. Other benefits include allowing the developer to arrange the resources on disk based on their usage. For example, all of the textures used in a level could sit in a single package, allowing for easy installation of new levels with all of the dependencies included. Console games with disc-based access need to consider the layout of the files on the physical disc, and often optimize for the reading patterns of a DVD or Blu-Ray drive.

Once you have a way to access the file from disk (either through an access layer or direct) you need to look at ways of loading and parsing the data. One common method used in games is to convert all data to a serialized format that can be easily read by the resource system. This allows for extra speed when loading because you don't need to parse generic content files, and makes it easier to secure your data and load it in. The **Microsoft XNA Framework** has a great example of this in the content pipeline, where `ContentProcessors` and `ContentImporters` work at the build stage to create the serialized file from source data. These files then represent **serialized** versions of the final objects used in the game, and using a little bit of reflection or an easily written `ContentReader`, a file can be loaded at runtime quickly and easily. This entire system allows the developer to load a file by specifying the resulting type and the path to the serialized file, with all of the loading happening behind the scenes.

 Reflection allows you to inspect classes, interfaces, fields, and methods at runtime. This allows you to write code that can dynamically create and interact with classes that you do not know about at compile time.

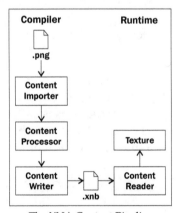

The XNA Content Pipeline

The point of this system is to have a way to re-use loaded data. This is done through the implementation of a **cache**, which can be simple or complex, depending on the needs of the game. If you consider the amount of memory and video RAM available to gamers today you'll see that smaller games can quite easily cache everything in memory and have no issues. If you're writing a larger game with a lot of graphics and audio assets, or you're writing for a limited platform such as a phone, you may find that you need to be a bit smarter about the lifetime of the resource and how you manage loading in content to ensure you do not exceed memory limits.

Commercial engines such as Unreal Engine use streaming technology to load in the content in the background while the user plays the game, avoiding the need for loading screens whenever new content appears. This also allows for the resources to be unloaded if the memory is almost full. Other options include controlling the size of the assets in a single level and unloading the assets when loading a new level; or keeping the assets that are shared and only unloading what isn't used.

If you bring all of this together you can build a robust, re-usable resource manager that will really help you with your game development. That is too big for this book though, so for our simple game we will just implement a simple `std::map` in the renderer that handles caching textures for us based on their filenames.

Culling

Having too much in the game world at once can reduce the frame rate of a game. We need a way to manage what is displayed to ensure we aren't drawing unnecessary objects. By drawing every single sprite, even the sprites and objects outside of the visible area (above, below, behind, or on either side), we waste a lot of time that could be spent drawing a new frame and giving a better experience. To resolve this, renderers often implement a method of culling to only draw what is visible. Essentially this is a glorified search algorithm, designed to search the scene for only the visible objects, and draw those while ignoring everything else. You could do this by iterating through a list and checking if each sprite is in the camera's view, but if you're working with many sprites you will soon waste CPU time going through every sprite every frame.

To resolve this, **acceleration structures** were invented that consider the position of the object and allow for coarse grained culling of entire batches, reducing the load on the CPU. In 3D one of the best known structures is called a **Binary Space Partition Tree** (BSP Tree). Here, the scene is constantly split in half, forming a tree structure until a threshold is met, usually a maximum number of objects in a node.

Another option is the **Quad-Tree**, which splits the scene into four sections at a time; however, unlike the BSP Tree, the Quad-Tree needs to be aligned to a grid (when splitting in half, you can place the split anywhere). This is great for static objects, and once constructed makes it very quick and easy to search through as you can remove entire branches of the tree by determining which ones are visible.

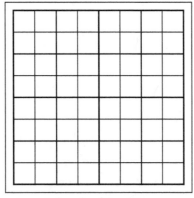

A three-level Quad-Tree

In our game we won't need any culling because if anything leaves the screen it will be destroyed.

Implementation

To get started with the implementation, we need to consider the code we already have. The texture class implemented in the previous chapters hold the image we want to render, but it also contains a position to render at. Normally this might not be an issue but if we want to cache the texture, we need to separate that position variable so that we can re-use the texture object. To do this, we'll create a new class named sprite, and move the position property to that class, as well as add a shared pointer to a texture so that the sprite can be linked with a loaded image. For reference, here are the class definitions for the `Sprite` and `Texture`.

```
class Sprite
{
private:
  std::shared_ptr<Texture> _tex;

public:

  XMFLOAT2 Position;
```

```
        float Rotation;
        XMFLOAT2 Scale;
        XMFLOAT2 Origin;
        bool Visible;

        Sprite(void);
        ~Sprite(void);

        void SetTexture(std::shared_ptr<Texture> tex);
        void Draw(std::shared_ptr<SpriteBatch> sb);

        XMFLOAT2 GetSize() { return _tex->GetTextureSize(); };
    };
    class Texture
    {
    private:
        std::wstring _path;
        Microsoft::WRL::ComPtr<ID3D11Resource> _tex;
        Microsoft::WRL::ComPtr<ID3D11ShaderResourceView> _srv;

        DirectX::XMFLOAT2 _size;

    public:
        XMFLOAT2 GetTextureSize() { return _size; }

        void Draw(std::shared_ptr<DirectX::SpriteBatch> batch, XMFLOAT2
    &pos, float rotation, XMFLOAT2 &scale, XMFLOAT2 &origin = XMFLOAT2(0,
    0));
        void Load(Microsoft::WRL::ComPtr<ID3D11Device> device);

        Texture(std::wstring &path);
    };
```

Now let's look at how we can make use of this with a renderer that will manage the texture cache and rendering. Start off by creating a singleton in the same style as the InputManager we created earlier, and name it Renderer.

In this class we need to manage three things: the active sprite batch for rendering, the texture cache, and the list of sprites to be rendered. I'll refer to them as _ sb, _texCache, and _sprites, respectively. We'll also keep a reference to the ID3D11Device1 so that we can load textures. Alongside that, add an Initialize method that takes a ComPtr to ID3D11DeviceContext1 and ID3D11Device1.

```
    void Initialise(Microsoft::WRL::ComPtr<ID3D11DeviceContext1>
    context, Microsoft::WRL::ComPtr<ID3D11Device1> device);
```

The initialize method itself is pretty simple; we just keep track of the device, and create the `SpriteBatch` as we did in *Chapter 2, Drawing 2D Sprites*.

```
void Renderer::Draw()
{
  _sb->Begin();

  for (auto sprite : _sprites)
    sprite->Draw(_sb);

  _sb->End();
}
```

The `Draw` method is similar to what we created before, but in this case we loop through each of the Sprites in our vector between starting and stopping the `SpriteBatch`. The big part of this class, however, is the `CreateSprite` method, which we will use to create the sprite objects and ensure they're in the rendering list for display.

```
std::shared_ptr<Sprite> Renderer::CreateSprite(std::wstring &path)
{
  auto sprite = std::make_shared<Sprite>();
  auto tex = _texCache[path];
  if (tex == nullptr)
  {
    tex = std::make_shared<Texture>(path);
    tex->Load(_device);
    _texCache[path] = tex;
  }
  sprite->SetTexture(tex);
  _sprites.push_back(sprite);
  return sprite;
}
```

The two goals of this method are

1. Create the `Sprite` using the texture cache.
2. Add the `Sprite` to the rendering list.

This is also where we have all of the code for the really simple texture cache that we will be using. We use a simple `std::map` to store the textures, using the path as the key; that way we know we'll get the same texture because it will have the same path. Check for the texture and, if it doesn't exist, create it and load the texture from disk before adding it into the cache and the sprite. Once we have a texture, from the cache or disk, just add the sprite to our `_sprites` list that we use to easily loop through and render every instance.

Now it's time to use this renderer in our game and finally see the results of our structure and input system in action. Begin by calling `Renderer::Initialise` inside `Game::LoadContent` and `Renderer::Draw` inside `Game::Render`. This is all we need to do to hook the rendering system up to the game. Now we just need to create these sprites and we can try out our work. To do that, we need to fill in the `Ship::LoadTexture` method and add in a `std::shared_ptr` to a `Sprite` object to store the actual sprite.

```
void Ship::LoadTexture(std::wstring &path)
{
  _sprite = Renderer::GetInstance()->CreateSprite(path);
  _sprite->Position = _position;
  _sprite->Rotation = _rotation;
  _sprite->Scale = _scale;

  auto texSz = _sprite->GetSize();
  texSz.x /= 2.0f;
  texSz.y /= 2.0f;
  _sprite->Origin = texSz;
}
```

Most of the work done in this method involves copying over the current transformation properties to the sprite, as well as setting the origin of the sprite to the centre of the image. Now if everything is connected up properly you should be able to build and run the game to see your player ship (which can be moved with the controls you set) and enemies appearing from the right side of the screen every five seconds, unless you specified a different interval. The enemies should also move towards the left side of the screen.

So the enemies move towards the player, and then pass right through. This is where we need to add in a collision system to check when the enemies crash into the player, and later on when the bullets hit the enemies.

Collision detection

A collision system manages all of the calculations required to add a basic level of physics to your game by allowing objects to collide with each other and have some gameplay or visual effect. The key role of the collision system is to determine if a collision has occurred (collision detection). However, it may also be in charge of the response to a collision, depending on the needs of the game. In some cases, that is handled elsewhere and the collision system can be dedicated to detecting the collision and letting another system handle the response.

There are a lot of different ways to manage and run a collision system, but as usual with games you just need to stick to whatever gets the job done to your requirements. In this case we're not going to go and implement fancy acceleration structures such as the **Quad-Trees** mentioned in the renderer section, but remember there are just as many structures and techniques out there to make the best collision system possible.

I also mentioned that collision is part of physics. As a great benefit, most physics middleware packages contain collision libraries that will handle the complicated stuff for you, so as long as you understand what is happening and what you need, you can easily add in realistic collisions and physical reactions with minimal effort using libraries such as **box2d** or **Havok**.

In the case of this game, we need to consider which collision shapes will be necessary to implement the system. Thankfully we only need one type, the rectangle, which simplifies the work needed.

Rectangle collision

Rectangle collision in 2D involves checking if two rectangles overlap or contain each other. As shown in the following diagram, there are three different scenarios that need to be detected, and simpler checks will simply combine them all into a single true/false value; however, collision detection can be extended to specify which state the collision is (or isn't) in.

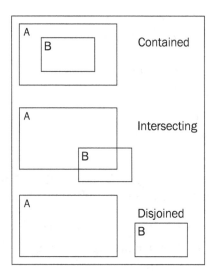

So let's create the `RectangleCollider` class that will handle the collision detection.

```
class RectangleCollider
{
public:
  RectangleCollider() : Enabled(true), Position(0,0), Size(0,0) {};

  bool Enabled;
  XMFLOAT2 Position;
  XMFLOAT2 Size;

  RectangleCollider(XMFLOAT2 topLeft, XMFLOAT2 size);
  bool CollidesWith(RectangleCollider *b);

  float X1();
  float X2();
  float Y1();
  float Y2();
};
```

Most of this is straightforward, but we also have some helper methods down the bottom, which provide the top-left and bottom right-corners of the rectangle as their individual components for use in the algorithm.

The main method we need to implement is the `RectangleCollider::CollidesWith` method.

```
bool RectangleCollider::CollidesWith(RectangleCollider *b)
{
  bool test1 = X1() < b->X2();
  bool test2 = X2() > b->X1();
  bool test3 = Y1() < b->Y2();
  bool test4 = Y2() > b->Y1();
  return test1 && test2 && test3 && test4;
}
```

Here we run four tests and if all pass we can say that rectangle A is inside or overlapping B. This is done by checking the following conditions:

- The left side of A is always inside or to the left of B
- The right side of A is always inside or to the right of B
- The top of A is always inside or above B
- The bottom of A is always inside or below B

One assumption made by this system is that we are working in a 2D plane, where Y increases towards the bottom of the screen. If you're working with a traditional Cartesian co-ordinate system where Y increases towards the top of the screen, adjust the algorithm accordingly.

 For a great demo of this collision technique, visit `http://silentmatt.com/rectangle-intersection/`.

Now we need to add this in to the game so that when enemies collide with the player or leave the play area they are destroyed. To do this we will add a `RectangleCollider` to the `Ship` class, and create it in the constructor. The next step is to ensure that we update the `RectangleCollider::Position` property each time the ship moves but be careful to offset it to the top left corner of the image rather than just the position of the ship. We do this to ensure that the bounding rectangle always contains the ship, even when moving. Remember that we render the ship with an origin in the centre of the image, and the collider doesn't know about this. Here's an example of the code we need to add to `Ship::LoadTexture` to set up the collider:

```
_collider->Position = XMFLOAT2(_position.x - _sprite->Origin.x, _
position.y - _sprite->Origin.y);
_collider->Size = _sprite->GetSize();
```

As you can see, we use the position of the ship, but remove the offset created by the origin before setting the position of the collider. We also need to set the size of the collider to the size of the texture once it has loaded.

Now we need to perform the collision checks. The best way to do this right now is to add this to the Game class during our update loop. We'll add a new method called `ProcessCollisions` that will be called at the end of the `Update` method. We also need to determine if the enemies are still on screen, and to do this we will test if an enemy is inside a collider that represents the screen. Create a `RectangleCollider` and create it inside `Game::LoadContent` by setting the size of the collider to the screen size – but make sure to add one to the width so that the enemies aren't destroyed as soon as they spawn outside of the screen.

```
void Game::ProcessCollisions()
{
  auto playerCollider = _player->GetCollider();
  for (auto enemy : _enemies)
  {
    if (enemy->GetIsAlive())
    {
      auto enemyCollider = enemy->GetCollider();
```

```
        // Check if collided against the player
        if (enemyCollider->CollidesWith(playerCollider))
          enemy->SetIsAlive(false);
        // Check if the enemy has exited the play area
        if (!enemyCollider->CollidesWith(_bounds))
          enemy->SetIsAlive(false);
      }
    }
  }
```

In here we simply go through each enemy and if it is active we do two things. First we check if the enemy has collided with the player and, if it has, we destroy the enemy. Later on we'll add in a gameplay consequence for this.

The other thing we need to do is to check if the enemy is still inside the screen. This is done by checking if the enemy no longer collides with the screen collider and destroying it if it is outside.

So now we have the enemies flying towards the player and disappearing when they reach the left side of the screen or when they touch the player. We have one more collision feature to add before we finish up the gameplay.

When the player, moves up or down on the screen they can currently move outside of the screen, which we don't want. We don't need to do a lot here, and the best place to put this detection is inside the `Player` class. However you could still classify this as collision detection.

Inside `Player::Update` we need to update the movement code to look like the following:

```
if (_actionMoveDown->IsTriggered())
{
  Move(ShipDirection::Down, deltaTime);
  auto bottom = _collider->Position.y + _collider->Size.y;
  if (bottom > screenHeight)
    MoveTo(_position.x, screenHeight - _sprite->Origin.y);
}
else if(_actionMoveUp->IsTriggered())
{
  Move(ShipDirection::Up, deltaTime);
  if (_collider->Position.y < 0)
    MoveTo(_position.x, _sprite->Origin.y);
}
```

The parts you need to focus on here are the lines after the Move calls. If the player moves down, we need to make sure the bottom of the image doesn't cross below the screen. When moving up, we need to ensure the vertical position doesn't go below zero, or the top of the screen. If the player goes past any of these points we just lock the player to the edge of the screen until it moves in the opposite direction.

Now if you run the game, the player should be locked within the screen and enemies should spawn and move to the left until they pass the edge of the screen or hit the player.

Fighting for score

We've got a lot in place; now we just need to put these parts together in another way to add in some more gameplay, in the form of bullets that will be fired at the enemy.

Let's begin by creating a Bullet class; this will allow us to control the movement of the bullet and easily manage lifetime and damage.

```
class Bullet
{
private:
  RectangleCollider *_collider;
  std::shared_ptr<Sprite> _sprite;
  bool _isAlive;

public:
  int Damage;

  Bullet();
  ~Bullet();

  void Load();

  RectangleCollider* GetCollider() { return _collider; }

  void SetPosition(XMFLOAT2 topleft);
  void MoveForward(float deltaTime);

  void Destroy();
  void Respawn();
  bool GetIsAlive();
};
```

There's quite a bit in here, but most of it you have seen before. We need a `Sprite` and a collider for the bullet so that we can display it and easily check for collisions with the enemy. We use `SetPosition` to set the initial position when we spawn the bullet, and `MoveForward` to let the bullet handle moving in the right direction and updating both the collider and the sprite.

`Destroy` and `Respawn` both manage the `_isAlive` variable and ensure that the sprite is only visible when the bullet is alive. `Bullet::Load` will load the texture located at `textures\bullet.DDS` in the same way as the `Player` or `Enemy`.

Now we need to integrate the bullet class into the game. As we want the bullet fire to be continuous we need a different way of caching and managing the bullets. For this we'll use a pool system, as mentioned earlier. Add the following declarations to `Game.h`:

```
std::list<Bullet*> _bullets;
std::queue<Bullet*> _bulletPool;
Bullet* CreateBullet();
```

Here we'll use the list to manage the bullets that exist, and the queue to allow us to cache "dead" bullets that can be reused later. We'll encapsulate this management functionality inside `CreateBullet`, which looks like this:

```
Bullet* Game::CreateBullet()
{
  Bullet *b;
  if (_bulletPool.size() == 0)
  {
    b = new Bullet();
    b->Damage = 100;
    b->Load();
  }
  else
  {
    b = _bulletPool.front();
    _bulletPool.pop();
  }

  b->Respawn();
  _bullets.push_back(b);
  return b;
}
```

Here we check if there are any bullets in the stand-by pool and if there aren't any we create a new one, set the damage value, and load the sprite for it. Once that's done, we can call respawn to ensure it is "alive" and then add it to the active bullets list. We'll use this in our `Game::Update` method to create new bullets based on a firing timer we implement inside the `Player` class.

But first let's add the code to update the bullets and manage the cache. Inside update, near the top, add the following code:

```
std::vector<Bullet*> garbage;
for (auto bullet : _bullets)
{
  if (bullet->GetIsAlive())
  {
    bullet->MoveForward(deltaTime);
  }
  else
  {
    _bulletPool.push(bullet);
    garbage.push_back(bullet);
  }
}
for (auto toRemove : garbage)
  _bullets.remove(toRemove);
```

Here we go through all of the active bullets and check if they are alive. If they are, we just move them forward using `Bullet::MoveForward`. If not, we need to add them to the available pool and also flag them for deletion from the active list using a temporary vector that indicates the garbage to clean up.

This is similar to the Mark and Sweep garbage collection style. First the items to be destroyed are marked for deletion during an initial pass, and once that is complete they are deleted in one go.

Once this update is complete we simply go through all of the items in the temporary garbage vector and remove them from the active list.

Near the bottom of the same `Game::Update` method, add the following code:

```
if (_player->CanFire())
{
  auto b = CreateBullet();
  b->SetPosition(_player->GetPosition());
}
```

Here we use a helper method that we're about to define called `CanFire` to check if the player can fire a new shot. If they can, we use the `CreateBullet` helper from before to generate (or retrieve) a new bullet, which we can then reposition, ready to move during the next update.

`Player::CanFire` manages the reload time to allow us to have a delay between individual shots while we use this continuous firing system—after all, we don't want 30 or 60 shots every single second!

```
bool Player::CanFire()
{
  auto result = _sinceLastShot > ReloadTime;
  if (result)
    _sinceLastShot = 0;
  return result;
}
```

In a similar fashion to the enemy spawning system in Game, we use a variable named `_sinceLastShot` to track the amount of time since the previous shot. This we update in `Player::Update` using the delta time. If the player can fire, we assume that the caller (`Game`) will fire, and reset the timer to zero, making it ready to count towards the next shot. This would be the perfect location to add in another action that allows the user to press a button to fire.

Now we need to make these bullets do something. Back in `Game` you will remember we have a method for managing collisions named `ProcessCollisions`.

```
for (auto bullet : _bullets)
{
  if (bullet->GetIsAlive())
  {
    if (!bullet->GetCollider()->CollidesWith(_bounds))
    {
      bullet->Destroy();
    }
    else
    {
      for (auto enemy : _enemies)
      {
        if (enemy->GetIsAlive() && bullet->GetCollider()-
>CollidesWith(enemy->GetCollider()))
        {
```

```
        enemy->Damage(bullet->Damage);
        bullet->Destroy();
        if (!enemy->GetIsAlive())
          _playerScore += 50;
      }
    }
  }
 }
}
```

We need to add a loop at the bottom of this to go through each bullet in existence and check against all of the living enemies to see if there has been a collision, or alternatively check if the bullet has left the screen. In both cases we want to destroy the bullet; however, if the bullet hits an enemy we want to damage the enemy using the damage value specified by Bullet::Damage. The code inside Enemy will handle destruction if it runs out of health. In this example each bullet instantly kills; however, if you remember, when we created each bullet we set the Damage value. Feel free to tweak the value as well as the health of the enemy to find the balance you want.

Now you should be able to run the game and see the bullets emerge from the player and hit the enemies, destroying them. We have gameplay in place, but these kinds of games really rely on one other little feature to make them better: Scoring.

Now that we have everything in place, implementing scoring is really easy. We need to track the score, and add/remove from it based on different events that happen in the game, as well as display the score by adding some text rendering from *Chapter 2, Drawing 2D Sprites* to the Renderer.

First we need to add an integer score variable to Game; I named mine _playerScore. Ensure you set this to zero in the constructor so the player doesn't start with a random score from some uninitialized memory — that would be confusing. There are three points at which the player can gain or lose score, and they all happen after a collision, so the best place to adjust the score is inside ProcessCollisions.

Here you can choose your own values but, as an example, if the enemy collides with the player we levy a penalty of 1000 points. If the enemy exits the screen on the left the penalty is 100 points, and if the player destroys an enemy we award him or her 500 points. We'll use a helper method called AddScore to allow us to manage this by passing positive or negative amounts to be added to the score. This allows us to separate out the score update so that we can be prepared for the next part.

Now we need to display this score to the player, to give them some feedback so they know where they stand. First we need to add some text functionality to the renderer. To do this, we're going to create a new class named `TextBlock`, which will store the `Text`, `Position`, and `Color` that will be used along with the `SpriteFont` to draw the string we want.

```
class TextBlock
{
public:
  std::wstring Text;
  DirectX::XMFLOAT2 Position;
  DirectX::XMFLOAT4 Color;

  TextBlock() : Text(L""), Position(0, 0),
Color(DirectX::Colors::White) {};
};
```

Now we need to add a `SpriteFont`, and a vector of `TextBlocks` to the `Renderer`. We will load the `SpriteFont` just like in *Chapter 2, Drawing 2D Sprites*, but remember that we need the path, so we need to add a new parameter to Initialize, and then set that to the path of our `.font` file. We'll also create a new helper method in Renderer named `CreateText` that creates a new `TextBlock` and adds it to the `TextBlock` vector.

Now add the following code to the `Draw` method, after you draw the sprites (but before you call `_sb->End()`:

```
for (auto text : _text)
{
  auto colVec = DirectX::XMLoadFloat4(&(text->Color));
  _font->DrawString(_sb.get(), text->Text.data(), text->Position,
colVec);
}
```

Once we have that we can add some code to the `Draw` method before we end the `SpriteBatch` to draw each item in the `TextBlock` vector using the stored data.

Now let's return to the `Game` class in Game.cpp.

```
_scoreText = Renderer::GetInstance()->CreateText();
_scoreText->Position.x = m_renderTargetSize.Width - 500;
_scoreText->Position.y = 50;
_scoreText->Text = std::wstring(L"Score: 0");
```

Inside Game::LoadContent we'll create a new TextBlock that will be named _
scoreText and keep a reference to that so that we can update the Text property
inside the AddScore method. We will position the score on the right-hand side of the
screen so that the player sprite doesn't clash with it, and give it an initial text so that
it doesn't suddenly appear later in the game.

```
_scoreText->Text = L"Score: " + std::to_wstring(_playerScore);
```

This line needs to be added to the AddScore method to update the score string. We
can use to_wstring from the <string> header to help construct the string, ready
for use.

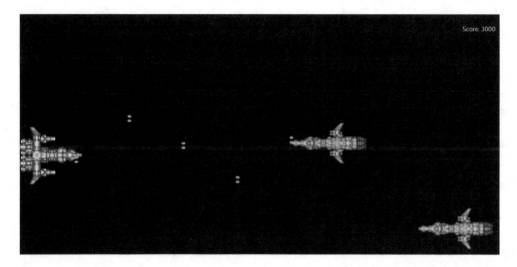

Summary

In this chapter we took what we learned in the previous two chapters and built
up a collection of systems that allow us to implement the actual gameplay of the
game. We went from some sample code to test out rendering and input, and added
structure so that we can easily define input actions that can be triggered by multiple
devices. We restructured our rendering so that the textures can be re-used and
centralized the drawing functionality so that with one call we can draw every sprite
and piece of text required.

From there we added in gameplay by adding in the Player, Enemy, and Bullet
classes and the supporting Ship class. We added the code required to spawn new
enemies and fire new bullets, an also looked at the caching techniques we could use
to manage both of those.

Then we added destruction with a simple collision system that allowed us to easily manage collision shapes that allow us to make collision detection faster. This was the big piece of the puzzle needed to lock in the gameplay and allow the player to have an effect on the enemy, as well as a consequence for not dealing with them.

Through all of this you have hopefully gained an understanding of just some of the systems required for games, and the plentiful set of tools and options available to you when building them. Remember that there is no single way to do it. Every game is unique and choosing the best tool for the job, even if it means new code, is the best way to go. Consider performance, but be realistic. You may have some inefficient code, but if it is only called once a frame then it might not be worth wasting time on it. Also consider that implementing complex but "efficient" algorithms can often perform worse if you've got a controlled small set of objects.

There are hundreds of ways to make a game, and thousands upon thousands of resources available in print and online to help you. As you build you will refine and learn, but remember that the heart of the game is in the gameplay and the fun, not the amazing memory manager that takes 5 days to implement. (Although that's a cool thing to work on as well.)

Next steps

From here, look at the different values we defined in this chapter: the speeds, respawn, and firing rates and the damage of the bullets. Play around with those values, tweak and change them to find a game that feels nice to play. You can even randomize the spawn time between enemies using rand() or some other random number generator. Variety is awesome, and mixing things up (or even adding new enemies) can really help a game.

In the next chapter we're going to take this simple concept into a new area with the introduction of multiplayer. We'll add in some simple local co-operative play to allow someone else to join you in this space battle, and you'll see Windows 8 features that make it easier to find and create games using the new Proximity and Networking APIs.

5
Tilting the World

We now have a game in place. The user can fly up and down the screen, shooting at the enemies and destroying them for points. Barring some polish this could be considered complete; however, there are very many benefits that come with a Windows Store app, so over the next few chapters we will take a look at some of them and consider what we can use to improve our game and make it just a bit more unique.

Sensors such as the **accelerometer**, **gyroscope**, and **GPS** allow many new opportunities for games and applications in today's mobile world. By adding in GPS support you can give games the ability to know where the player is, enabling augmented reality or location-based game design that enters new territory. Adding in orientation sensors allows for richer input for games, and even new classes of games that take advantage of the positioning of the device in newer ways.

Over the course of this chapter we will look at the different sensors available to you in Windows 8, such as the following:

- Orientation
- Accelerometer
- Gyroscope (or gyrometer)
- Compass
- Inclinometer

We'll look at small code snippets to see how to access and use these sensors using the WinRT libraries, and integrate the orientation sensors into our game as a new input mechanism—allowing the players to tilt their devices to move their ships across the screen.

Before you begin, the event-based methods for accessing sensor and other device readings may occur on a separate thread — if this is a potential issue for your game, be sure to implement some form of synchronization.

Orientation

There are multiple sensors that can be used independently or in combination to get the orientation of a device. Many modern mobile PCs, from tablets to even laptops have some or all of these sensors built-in. WinRT allows access to the individual sensors, as well as a nice Orientation Sensor API that combines all of the provided data and does the math required to give you the angles you want in a simpler form. It's up to you what you use, depending on how much information you require.

Let's take a look at how to work with each sensor individually, and then look at the Orientation Sensor API, which takes data from all of these and gives you the information you need, saving you a lot of time.

Accelerometer

The accelerometer is a sensor that detects the direction and acceleration of the device. This can be used to determine if the device is moving, but sometimes it is used to determine the gravity direction to provide a reference to other sensors and determine orientation.

For example, if the accelerometer is providing values indicating movement towards the bottom of the device, close to the acceleration due to gravity, you know that the device is upright.

There are two methods of accessing accelerometer data within your game. The first is to listen for events providing updated accelerometer values. The second is to poll for the values and, depending on the structure of your game, the latter may be the more desirable option.

To work with the accelerometer, we need to use the `Accelerometer` class within the `Windows::Devices::Sensors` namespace. To create an instance of this class, just use the following code:

```
Accelerometer^ accelerometer = Accelerometer::GetDefault();
```

This will give us the default accelerometer, ready for use. If no accelerometer exists, we'll get a `nullptr` value, which should be handled before anything happens.

Once you have the accelerometer, you need to set a reporting interval that fits your needs. The **reporting interval** defines the amount of time between each update of the accelerometer values. With this we can increase or reduce the frequency of the updates and, if we're using events for data retrieval, we can adjust how frequently they occur. The accelerometer will have a minimum reporting interval, so use that information when deciding on your reporting interval by checking the `accelerometer->MinimumReportInterval`. Once you've decided on the interval, you can set it with the following line of code:

```
accelerometer->ReportInterval = desiredReportInterval;
```

Now all that you need to do is register an event handler for the `accelerometer->ReadingChanged` event, as follows:

```
accelerometer->ReadingChanged::add(
  ref new TypedEventHandler<
  Accelerometer^, AccelerometerReadingChangedEventArgs^>
(
    this,
    &MyClass::ReadingChanged
  ));
```

This particular event can be set with a `TypedEventHandler` that has the `Accelerometer` and `AccelerometerReadingChangedEventArgs` parameters.

Now you need the event handler method, and in this case we've named it `ReadingChanged`. The event system provides access to the `Accelerometer` object, as well as the event arguments, which contain the readings for that event, and this is the object you need to use to get the values you want.

`AccelerometerReadingChangedEventArgs` is a simple class that contains a single property named `Reading`, which is an `AccelerometerReading`. The reading itself is pretty simple; the class has the following properties that you can use to get the information you need:

```
property double AccelerationX;
property double AccelerationY;
property double AccelerationZ;
property Windows::Foundation::DateTime Timestamp;
```

Just read the values directly out of the `Reading` object to get the information you need.

When you're done, just remove your event handler from the `ReadingChanged` event (keep the token you get when you set the handler) and set the `ReportInterval` to `0`, which notifies Windows that the resources can be released.

As you can see, this is really simple; let's take a look at what you need to do to poll for these events, in case you want the game play to be controlled by the accelerometer function.

To poll for the values we still need to get the default accelerometer and set up the `ReportInterval` as we did earlier; however, instead of setting an event to retrieve the reading, we will call the following function:

```
auto reading = accelerometer->GetCurrentReading();
```

This will give us the last reading (based on the `ReportInterval`) that Windows has in an `AccelerometerReading` object. This is exactly the same class that is provided by the `Reading` property inside `AccelerometerReadingChangedEventArts`. Ensure that you check if your reading is null before trying to access it, as if there is an issue with the accelerometer you may not receive a reading.

Shaking things up a bit

The accelerometer is a special sensor that can also determine movement, which can be useful if you want to implement some form of shake detection. This is common enough within standard apps that WinRT has a system that does the shake detection for you. The shake detection system is only accessible through the event system; however, you don't need to set any intervals, just hook into the `Accelerometer::Shaken` event to know when the device has been shaken.

As usual you need to get the default accelerometer, and once you have that you need to bind a `TypedEventHandler` to the `Shaken` event, specifying the `Accelerometer^` and `AccelerometerShakenEventArgs` as template types, as shown:

```
accelerometer->Shaken::add(
  ref new TypedEventHandler<
Accelerometer^, AccelerometerShakenEventArgs^>
(
this,
&MyClass::Shaken
));
```

All you get from that event call is the accelerometer and the event arguments, which just contain a timestamp. The focus here is on simplicity, so you can tell Windows that you want to know when the user shakes the device, and you don't need raw values or details.

Remember that these are not mutually exclusive, and you can use any of the three methods in any combination. As you will see, the focus of the API is to make it easy to get the information you want, and in doing so you have the freedom to do what you need to do.

Spinning with gyros

That's how you work with an accelerometer; let's look at how to work with a gyroscope. Gyroscopes help to measure the orientation of the device by providing the angular velocity (rotation speed) of the device. If you track the angular velocity, you can determine how much the device is being rotated (in degrees per second) and find the current rotation of the device.

In Windows 8 the gyro is accessed through the `Gyrometer` class, inside the `Windows::Devices::Sensors` namespace, as shown. You can access the readings using events, or through a polling method similar to the accelerometer.

```
Gyrometer^ gyro = Gyrometer::GetDefault();
```

To access the gyro you first need to get the default instance, done by calling the `GetDefault()` method. Once you have this you can set the reporting interval and then register for an event handler or use the `GetCurrentReading()` method to poll the device. This is shown in the following code snippet:

```
// Setup
Gyrometer^ gyro = Gyrometer::GetDefault();
if (gyro != nullptr)
gyro->ReportInterval = gyro->MinimumReportInterval > 16 ?
  gyro->MinimumReportInterval : 16;

// Shut-down
gyro->ReportInterval = 0;
```

The given code shows the setup and shutdown code for the `Gyrometer` class, which is necessary for both forms of data retrieval. We retrieved the default gyro and checked if the gyro exists on the device by checking if the returned value is null. If a gyro does exist we will set the report interval in milliseconds, without going below the minimum report interval.

Finally, when we're ready to shut the device down, we will set the report interval to zero, which releases the resources and saves power. Now let's take a look at some examples of reading from the gyro:

```
gyro->ReadingChanged::add(
ref new TypedEventHandler<
Gyrometer^, GyrometerReadingChangedEventArgs^>
(
this,
&MyClass::ReadingChanged
));
```

Just as with the accelerometer, this sets the `Gyrometer` to report new readings (based on the `ReportInterval`) to the `ReadingChanged()` method. An example of that method looks like the following code snippet:

```
void MyClass::ReadingChanged(Gyrometer^ g,
GyrometerReadingChangedEventArgs^ args)
{
  GyrometerReading^ reading = args->Reading;
double velocityX = reading->AngularVelocityX;
double velocityY = reading->AngularVelocityY;
double velocityZ = reading->AngularVelocityZ;
}
```

Here we can retrieve the angular velocities as well as the timestamp, and make use of them as required. Now if we want to poll, as earlier, we just need to set up the code, and call the `gyro->GetCurrentReading()` method to retrieve the `GyrometerReading` object that contains the velocities.

Compass

Knowing the rotation of the device is great, but the values aren't relative to anything else. You don't know if the device is pointing North or South. This is where the compass (also known as the magnetometer) comes into play. Many devices have this sensor so you can usually rely on it for some basic but useful orientation information.

The Compass API in Windows 8 is very similar to both the accelerometer and the gyro. You get the `Compass` object through `GetDefault()`, and you can gather readings through events or polling after setting the `ReportInterval`.

The difference between these sensors really lies in the provided data. Both the accelerometer- and gyro-provided velocities are for each axis, so essentially when the device stops moving, the readings return to the idle values of the gravity vector for the accelerometer, or zero for the gyro. You need to put in the effort to track these sensors and update other values to get extra meaningful information out of them in most cases.

The compass does something different. Just like a physical compass, the one provided by the operating system provides values that indicate the rotation of the device, rather than a velocity that can settle. Inside the `CompassReading` class there are three values, the timestamp and two heading values that represent the heading relative to the Magnetic North and the geographic True North.

We have two values for a reason. The **Magnetic North** reading provides the direction to the Magnetic North pole of the Earth, which isn't quite the same as the North that you see on the maps. These instead use something called **True North**, or **Geographic North**, which represents the North Pole that the Earth rotates around. Both values are provided as `double` data type representing the degrees from their respective North poles (also known as bearing).

One thing to remember is that, just like a physical compass, the magnetometer can be affected by magnetic fields, such as those generated by speakers. If the compass is in an area of interference, we may get incorrect values from the device. Having some form of backup control in case the compass is unreliable (that the users can enable or disable) will help improve their experience.

Inclinometer

An inclinometer provides the yaw, pitch, and roll of the device in degrees, which is quite useful because it provides usable data without having to worry about calculating these values based on readings from the accelerometer, gyro, and compass. You'll see why not having this sensor isn't a big deal later on; however, if it is available you can get reasonably accurate readings easily, without having to go through any extra effort.

To get started using the inclinometer, you'll be doing most of the same work as the sensors that were mentioned earlier. Setup is done using the `Inclinometer::GetDefault()` method, and you will need to set the `ReportInterval` to start the sensor. Shutting this one down is just a matter of setting the `ReportInterval` to zero.

This device provides the following information from a reading:

```
property double PitchDegrees;
property double RollDegrees;
property double YawDegrees;
property DateTime Timestamp;
```

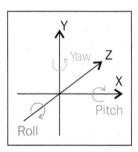

As shown in the preceding diagram, for this sensor the pitch refers to the rotation around the x axis (looking up and down). The roll refers to the rotation around the z axis, which extends away from the player, and the yaw refers to the rotation around the y axis.

Orientation for games

Aside from the inclinometer, you'll notice that all of the orientation sensors give values that may not be intuitive to use, and often require extra processing before you find them useful. WinRT has an API that draws data from all of the available sensors and does its best to give you useful rotation information that you can immediately make use of. As with the individual sensors, you can use this API in an event-based fashion, or you can poll for data.

 This process is called **sensor fusion**, and is available on many different platforms, including Windows Phone.

You can prepare this system using the same techniques as the individual sensors, by calling the `GetDefault()` method and setting the `ReportInterval` as well as the event handler, if required, by using the following type:

```
TypedEventHandler<
OrientationSensor^,
OrientationSensorReadingChangedEventArgs^>
```

The `OrientationSensorReadingChangedEventArgs` provides you with an `OrientationSensorReading` object that contains the following values:

```
property DateTime Timestamp;
property SensorQuaternion Quaternion;
property SensorRotationMatrix RotationMatrix;
```

There are some new types here that you may not have encountered before, in particular, the `SensorQuaternion`. A `Quaternion` in this context is a numeric representation of the rotation, in four components, XYZW. By representing the rotation in this form rather than the traditional RollPitchYaw or XYZ angles we can avoid some issues that occur, such as Gimbal Lock, where you lose an axis of rotation if the object rotates 90 degrees up or down.

The other type here is the `SensorRotationMatrix`, which is a 4 x 4 matrix containing the rotation values of the device, ready to be used in a 3D setting.

For more details on matrices and rotation in 3D, see the *Appendix, Adding the Third Dimension*.

This particular class is designed to help make game development using the sensors easier by providing the rotation information in a form that is useful to game developers—particularly those working in 3D. The representations provided by this class aren't as useful to us for a 2D game so we won't use them however, if you're working with a 3D game, this is an excellent system that provides readymade data for you to use.

Practice makes perfect

Now we'll take the most relevant sensor for our needs, the inclinometer, and use it to add in a new input method that uses the pitch of the device to move the ship up and down on the screen. We'll use the inclinometer because it provides the basic angles that we need to implement this input method, and this sensor is available on tablets like the Surface RT. The key thing to remember is that this is an optional input method, and you need to ensure you do the appropriate checks to not have any problems if the player is on a machine that does not support the sensor. You can restrict this if your game relies on the sensor—we will cover this in a later chapter.

We will start by creating a new trigger implementation that we will call the `InclinometerTrigger`. This will act similarly to our other triggers and will handle the polling of the inclinometer to get the latest values. This is shown in the code snippet that follows:

```
typedef enum
{
  Pitch,
  Roll,
  Yaw
} RotationAxis;

class InclinometerTrigger :
  public Trigger
{
private:
  Windows::Devices::Sensors::Inclinometer^ _inclinometer;
  RotationAxis _axis;
  float _lowerBound;
  float _upperBound;
```

```
public:
  InclinometerTrigger(void);
  ~InclinometerTrigger(void);

  virtual bool IsTriggered(InputManager*);
  void SetData(RotationAxis axis, float lowerBound, float upperBound);
};
```

This is the class declaration for the `InclinometerTrigger`. Here we need to define an enumeration to allow us to specify which rotation axis to check, and we will also store references to the inclinometer and the data defining the trigger condition.

We will run the following code inside the constructor:

```
// Inclinometer is in the Windows::Devices::Sensors namespace
_inclinometer = Inclinometer::GetDefault();
if (_inclinometer != nullptr)
  _inclinometer->ReportInterval =
_inclinometer->MinimumReportInterval;
```

Here we only update the `ReportInterval` if the inclinometer exists, and later on we'll check if the inclinometer has a value before trying to retrieve anything. This is important because Windows returns a `nullptr` if the device doesn't actually exist, and while we can just leave the trigger there doing nothing, we don't want the game to crash if the user is trying to run it on a machine without any sensors.

As with the other triggers, the real work happens inside the `InclinometerTrigger::IsTriggered()` method, as shown:

```
bool InclinometerTrigger::IsTriggered(InputManager *manager)
{
  if (_inclinometer == nullptr) return false;

  auto reading = _inclinometer->GetCurrentReading();
  if (reading == nullptr) return false;

  bool result = false;
  switch (_axis)
  {
  case Pitch:
    result = reading->PitchDegrees > _lowerBound && reading-
>PitchDegrees < _upperBound;
    break;

  case Yaw:
```

```
   result = reading->YawDegrees > _lowerBound && reading->YawDegrees
< _upperBound;
   break;

 case Roll:
   result = reading->RollDegrees > _lowerBound && reading-
>RollDegrees < _upperBound;
   break;
 }

 return result;
}
```

Here we will do our safety checks to see if the inclinometer exists, and if the value returned by it exists. As stated in the documentation, the operating system doesn't have to return a value, and this should be checked for.

Based on the requested axis, we will retrieve the angle and then do a simple bounds check to see if the angle is within the specified upper and lower bounds. If we are within those bounds, we can indicate that this has been triggered and our normal code will handle it from there.

The final touch comes from making use of this new trigger inside the Player class. Just create a new InclinometerTrigger as you did the rest of the triggers and set the data on it, as shown:

```
auto tiltDownTrigger =
_actionMoveDown->CreateTrigger<InclinometerTrigger>();
tiltDownTrigger->SetData(RotationAxis::Pitch, 5, 90);

auto tiltUpTrigger =
_actionMoveUp->CreateTrigger<InclinometerTrigger>();
tiltUpTrigger->SetData(RotationAxis::Pitch, -90, -5);
```

Here we created the triggers and set some thresholds. It would be annoying if the ship moved back and forth while the player tried to hold the device steady, so we use a ten degree threshold between 5 and -5 degrees that indicates that nothing should happen. This is done by specifying the bounds of the triggers from 5 to 90 degrees for movement down the screen, and -5 to -90 degrees for movement up the screen. Remember that we're doing numeric comparisons, so -5 is higher than -90 and should be arranged accordingly, otherwise the trigger will never be true.

Try it out now by deploying to a device that has sensors; if you have a tablet you should be able to use that. Also try running this on a standard PC or laptop without any sensors; you should not see any crashes and the game should behave as if the sensor code never existed.

Other sensors

In this section we'll take a look at the other sensors available in Windows 8 that can be useful for games. Whether they are used in conjunction with the other sensors or by themselves, these sensors can provide valuable data about the physical world. This context can be used for games that augment the world around the player and introduce new gameplay concepts that may not have been done before.

Light

One of the other sensors available for use is the **light** sensor. The light sensor is available on most tablet devices and provides an **illuminance** value that is usually used to adjust the screen brightness; however, any app or game can take advantage of this to provide different functionality. For example, a mapping application may use the illuminance value to determine if the phone is in sunlight and provides a different style of map that is easier to see. This could be done by games that use maps as well, or you might make a horror game that reacts to the light around the player, increasing immersion.

To set up the `LightSensor` object we will do the same thing as all of the previous sensors; we call the `LightSensor::GetDefault()` method and check if it exists by checking the returned value for a null pointer.

Assuming we have the sensor, we can retrieve the values using the event system by registering a `TypedEventHandler` that has a `LightSensor` and `LightSensorReadingChangedEventArgs` for its template arguments.

If we want to use the polling method, it's a simple matter of calling the `GetCurrentReading()` method when we need the data and making use of the data stored in the provided `LightSensorReading` object.

The `LightSensorReading` object provides us with two values, one for the timestamp included with all of the other readings, and one called `IlluminanceInLux`, which is a float that stores the lux reading.

Lux is a unit of measurement of the amount of visible light. As a reference, you can expect the indoor lighting to be of approximately 500 lux, while direct sunlight can be in the tens or hundreds of thousands. As with any of these sensor values, you will want to check the values you get and establish thresholds for input.

Locking on with a GPS

Although we know how to find the orientation of the device, we don't really know where it is in the world. This is where the **GPS** sensor comes into play. The GPS sensor (if installed) provides the latitude and longitude location of the machine, which we can use to determine where the device is and enable games that take advantage of that information.

Many games can use this information to provide a rich experience to the player, from augmented reality games through to spatial games that require you to be in certain physical locations. The increase in mobile platforms (phones and tablets) means that there has been an increase in this style of game, and as this is such a new occurrence there isn't a defined type of game or genre that can take advantage of this.

WinRT has a GPS API that allows for quick and easy access to your location; however, you need to remember that this functionality is limited by a location capability, which the user can opt out of for privacy reasons. To request this capability from the operating system, you need to set the **Location** capability in the application manifest, as shown in the screenshot that follows:

Capabilities:

☐ Documents Library

☐ Enterprise Authentication

☐ Internet (Client)

☐ Internet (Client & Server)

☑ Location

☐ Microphone

The operating system will handle seeking permission from the user to use their location, so you just need to check that box and confirm if you have the permission when you need it.

Similar to the sensors discussed earlier, there are two different ways to get access to the information: events and polling. Unlike the sensors, however, there isn't a `GetDefault()` method that gives you the one instance of the sensor. This means you need to create and maintain a reference to a `Geolocator` object that will handle the GPS functionality.

To get started with the event-based GPS data collection, create a new `Geolocator` using the `ref new Geolocator()` method. The `Geolocator` object has two changes that need to be tracked at all times: status and position. Either of these could change, and you need to track the status of the `Geolocator` to know if the position data provided is still good. To do this, we need to register with the `geolocator->PositionChanged` and `geolocator->StatusChanged` events. For these we will use the `TypedEventHandler`, just like the orientation sensors, and provide the following template arguments.

For the `PositionChanged` event, the arguments are as follows:

- `Geolocator`
- `PositionChangedEventArgs`

For the `StatusChanged` event, the arguments are the following:

- `Geolocator`
- `StatusChangedEventArgs`

Status

The status of the geolocator indicates if we can use the position data. Depending on when we receive the information, or what response the user provides when prompted for permission, we will be provided with a status from the `PositionStatus` enumeration. The values for the status are as follows:

- `Disabled`
- `Initializing`
- `NoData`
- `NotAvailable`
- `NotInitialized`
- `Ready`

The only value of status that will result in good position data is `PositionStatus::Ready`; however, based on the other values you can take certain actions.

If the user has declined permission, the value will be Disabled. If no device is available, NotAvailable will be set. If the value is NotInitialized, this means that for event-based applications, the PositionChanged event handler hasn't been set; you can ignore this if your code is still going to set that. Initializing indicates that the device is still trying to connect to the right number of satellites and may have a value in future, but for now there is no data. If the system has initialized but doesn't have any data yet, the NoData value will be provided, which just means that you should wait for a future update where it will transition to Ready.

When we receive a StatusChanged event, these values can be checked using the StatusChanged::Status property on the provided instance, which results in the given enumeration.

Position

Upon receipt of a PositionChanged event, the arguments parameter will contain a Position property, which is a Geoposition object. Inside this object is a CivicAddress property and a Coordinate property, the latter of which has the Geocoordinate type.

For a game, you probably won't make use of the CivicAddress property, as this contains the city, state, postal code, and country of the nearest property to the location. The Geocoordinate Position property will be more interesting.

You can retrieve the latitude and longitude of the position using the Latitude and Longitude properties, both of which are of double data type. You can also retrieve an accuracy value through the Accuracy property, which defines the radius of the circle in which the real location may lie. This should indicate to you that the GPS isn't always pinpoint, and depending on your needs you may want to handle an inaccurate position.

The Geocoordinate type also provides the Heading and Altitude values so that you can get a better idea of the user's location in 3D space. The Heading itself is provided relative to True North, just like the compass, and the Altitude is provided in meters, with its own Accuracy value to indicate the range of accuracy currently provided.

Polling

Polling for the geolocation is a bit different from the sensor system, which just provides the latest value. If you want to retrieve the location from the GPS, you need to initiate a request, which the GPS will try to fulfill as soon as possible. This means that you need to use an asynchronous method to access this data, using the Task APIs in WinRT.

To do this, we will create a `Geolocator` as was done earlier; however, when you want to retrieve a location value you need to create a new `task<Geoposition^>`, which handles calling the `geolocator->GetGeopositionAsync()` method. This will immediately return; however, you won't get any data out of it until the operation completes. You have two options here. You can use the blocking `task::wait()` call to wait for it to complete (not recommended, as it may cause performance hiccups), and then retrieve the `Geoposition` using the `task::get()` method. Alternatively, you can use the `task::then()` method to define some code that will run after the `Geoposition` is acquired, in which you can update your game using the location provided, as shown:

```
task<Geoposition^> task(geolocation->GetGeopositionAsync());
task.then([this](task<Geoposition^> getPosTask)
{
  Geoposition^ pos = getPosTask.get();
  // Do what you need to do with the position
};
```

As shown in the given code, you can create the task, pass in the `GetGeopositionAsync()` method, and call the `task::then()` method, which indicates what to do once the task returns. We can pass in a method to it; however, in this case I've used a lambda to inline the code.

Summary

So now we know how to add a whole new dimension of input to our game, by making use of devices and location data. We've learned how to work with the accelerometer, gyroscope, inclinometer, compass, orientation sensor, and GPS.

Through this new knowledge we've also added the ability to move the player's ship in the game with the inclinometer, adding in a unique method of input that enriches the game for players with capable devices.

Consider how using these increasingly available sensors can improve your game through unique input or information. Enhance your game design and make it unique. Take advantage of the power of the platform and make an awesome tablet game that still supports PCs and laptops even if they don't have these sensors.

Next steps

We have a mostly feature-complete game. Players can move around and shoot using standard controls as well as the sensors on mobile devices. There are other ways we can add to the game before we submit this to the store, and in the next chapter we'll add the simplest form of multiplayer: bragging and competing with friends through high scores. We'll look at how to take the achievements of the players and integrate some unique Windows 8 features, such as live tiles and the share charm, to let players brag about their score with friends and show off what they've done without even needing to enter the game.

6
Bragging Rights

Score is a major feature in most games. It is a way to compete with others without even meeting them. High score lists have always been the way to show your friends your score; however, with Windows 8 we can make that a little more direct with the integrated sharing and Live Tiles features. To do this we're going to need to make some changes, so that when the game ends the players have a chance to see their scores, and are prompted to share those scores – this allows us to control when the players can share and gives them a chance to do so without ruining their games. This stop in the action also allows us to register if they have new high scores and update the tiles that will display the scores for them, so we need to ensure we have this in place first. To do this we'll take advantage of the WinRT component system to make things easier for ourselves, and learn about how you can use this to develop components in one WinRT compliant language and consume them in another language.

Over the course of this chapter we'll take a look at the following topics:

- Game state and progression
- Adding a basic game over screen
- Sharing in Windows 8
- Share sources versus share targets
- What are Live Tiles?
- WinRT components

Let's start by setting up our game to add in these features by adding in a basic form of game state that allows the game to end. We'll take this further in the next chapter when we really need it to add networking. However, for now we'll just look at the basics and get what we need in place. We'll also take a look at WinRT components, which allow us to write components in other languages and use them within our main game with minimal performance impact. We'll use this to make it easier to work with the Live Tiles using C#; however, from this you can learn how to integrate components written in other languages with minimal effort.

Using the live tile system as an example, we will be able to understand how to use these components to access functionality written in other languages, and the benefits and downsides that result from using these components. Remember that all of the functionality developed in this chapter can be developed by only using C++; however, we need to look at one of the biggest developer features introduced in Windows 8, and what better time to do so.

Game state and progression

The main thing our game has been lacking so far is an end. The enemies never stop flying at the player and the player never dies because the only penalty for dying is a score penalty. To have a high score, we need an end where we can freeze the score and say the player has earned it. To do this, we need to add in a way to end the game when the player dies. In the next chapter we'll look at implementing a proper menu system, but for now we'll focus on adjusting our game so that it ends and displays a score to the player.

To get started we need to change our game so that it ends at some point. We'll do this by damaging the player when the enemy collides with the player ship. This has the added benefit of giving us a flag that indicates if the player is alive and therefore if the game is running or finished. Thankfully we already have this functionality in the Ship base class that the Player inherits from, so we can go ahead and use that. We also need to decide how many enemies can hit the player before the game ends. In the sample I chose four enemies, and so with a health value of 100 we need to apply 25 damages per collision to make this work. You may want to choose a health value of 4 and simply deduct one point of damage for each collision as well; it all depends on your game and how you want to present that to the player. For this sample we'll stick to the commonly used 100 hit-points value.

Inside the collision detection code between the player and enemies we need to remove the code that changes the score and replace it with a call to `_player->Damage(25)`, which will handle damaging the player. As it is game over when the player dies, we need to add a check to the update method, and stop processing game logic when the `_player->GetIsAlive()` returns false. To do this, simply wrap all of the code in `Game::Update` with that check.

If you run the game now, you should be able to crash into four enemies before everything abruptly pauses. Now we need to create a game over screen, and get rid of all of the graphics from our game. To do this we need to make some modifications to our renderer to allow us to re-add the game graphics at a later stage, as well as add in some methods to retrieve the sprites from the Ship and Bullet.

First add the following method to `Ship` and `Bullet`:

```
std::shared_ptr<Sprite> GetSprite() { return _sprite; }
```

Adjust as necessary to fit your sprite name. We need this to retrieve and re-add the sprites when the game is restarted.

Inside `Renderer` we need to add a couple of methods to extend our `Sprite` and `TextBlock` management.

```
void Renderer::ClearSprites()
{
  _sprites.clear();
}

void Renderer::AddSprite(std::shared_ptr<Sprite> sprite)
{
  _sprites.push_back(sprite);
}

void Renderer::ClearText()
{
  _text.clear();
}

void Renderer::AddText(TextBlock *text)
{
  _text.push_back(text);
}
```

Here we just need a way to mass clear all of the Sprites and TextBlocks, as well as a way to add them without creating new ones. This way we can re-add the player/enemy/bullet sprites during a game restart without destroying and recreating the `Sprite` objects. Once we have that in place we need to add two methods to our `Game` class: `ResetGame()` and `EndGame()`. There will manage the state changes within our game.

```
void Game::ResetGame()
{
  auto renderer = Renderer::GetInstance();
  renderer->ClearSprites();
  renderer->ClearText();

  renderer->AddSprite(_player->GetSprite());
  _player->Reset();
```

```
  for (auto e : _enemies)
  {
    e->SetIsAlive(false);
    renderer->AddSprite(e->GetSprite());
  }

  // Move all bullets in the pool to a list
  // where we can reset their sprites
  while (_bulletPool.size() > 0)
  {
    _bullets.push_back(_bulletPool.front());
    _bulletPool.pop();
  }

  for (auto b : _bullets)
  {
    renderer->AddSprite(b->GetSprite());
    b->Destroy();
    _bulletPool.push(b);
  }
  _bullets.clear();

  AddScore(-_playerScore);
  renderer->AddText(_scoreText);
}
```

This first method handles resetting the game to the original state. It clears out the renderer and replaces all of the sprites while ensuring all bullets are in the available pool for spawning when required. All enemies are destroyed as well to ensure they spawn properly and the player can start from scratch. We reset the player to ensure their his or her health is back to normal, and finally reset the score to zero using our helper function that ensures the text display is up-to-date.

The counterpart to this method is the `EndGame` method, which handles clearing the screen and displaying our simple Game Over screen.

```
void Game::EndGame()
{
  auto renderer = Renderer::GetInstance();
  renderer->ClearSprites();
  renderer->ClearText();

  if (_gameOverText == nullptr)
    _gameOverText = Renderer::GetInstance()->CreateText();
  else
```

```
    renderer->AddText(_gameOverText);

  _gameOverText->Text = std::wstring(
    L"Game Over\nTap anywhere to try again\nFinal Score: ")
    + std::to_wstring(_playerScore);
  auto size = renderer->MeasureText(_gameOverText);
  _gameOverText->Position.x =
    (m_renderTargetSize.Width / 2) - (size.x / 2);
  _gameOverText->Position.y =
    (m_renderTargetSize.Height / 2) - (size.y / 2);
}
```

Here we clear everything from the renderer and create a new `TextBlock` that will hold the message we want to display to the player. In this case we're simply informing them that the game is over, along with the score, and an invitation to tap the screen to continue playing.

We need to set the text each time to ensure the score is up-to-date, and once that is done we need to reposition the object so that it is in the center of the screen. To do this we will add a helper method to the `Renderer` class to help us get the size of the text block using the current font.

```
XMFLOAT2 Renderer::MeasureText(TextBlock *block)
{
  XMVECTOR sizeVec = _font->MeasureString(block->Text.data());
  XMFLOAT2 sizeResult = XMFLOAT2(0, 0);
  XMStoreFloat2(&sizeResult, sizeVec);
  return sizeResult;
}
```

`MeasureString` uses the `SpriteFont::MeasureString` command and extracts the `XMFLOAT2` object from the provided `XMVECTOR` to get the width and height of the string in the text block. Once we have that we can apply a simple bit of math to determine where the top-left of the text block should be so that the block is centered on the screen.

The last step is to call `EndGame` when the player dies. This can be done with a quick check of `_player->GetIsAlive()` after your call to `_player->Damage()` inside `Game::ProcessCollisions`, as shown:

```
if (enemyCollider->CollidesWith(playerCollider))
{
  enemy->SetIsAlive(false);
  _player->Damage(25);
  {
    EndGame();
```

```
        return;
    }
}
```

You should be able to run the game now and see that the game over screen appears after colliding with four enemies. Now we just need to create a new input action that lets us know when the player taps the screen, so that we can call ResetGame to start a new game. We already have most of the code in place for this, so we just need to apply what we've learned in previous chapters and create a new action that will handle this. Two input methods have been chosen for this action, a tap (or click with the mouse) and the start button on the Xbox 360 controller. The following code implements these inputs using our previously created input system:

```
_tapAction = InputManager::GetInstance()->CreateAction();

auto tapTrigger =
    _tapAction->CreateTrigger<PointerAxisBoundsTrigger>();

auto widthBounds = CreateAxisBounds(
    0,
    m_renderTargetSize.Width);
auto heightBounds = CreateAxisBounds(
    0,
    m_renderTargetSize.Height);
tapTrigger->SetData(
    &widthBounds,
    &heightBounds,
    KeyState::JustReleased);

auto startTrigger =
    _tapAction->CreateTrigger<GamepadButtonTrigger>();
startTrigger->SetData(
    GamepadButtons::Start,
    KeyState::JustReleased);
```

The only difference between this code and previous chapters is that I'm making use of both the X and Y axis in PointerAxisBoundsTrigger. This allows me to specify the entire screen as a potential touch location, and KeyState::JustReleased allows it to only trigger when the touch point (or mouse button) is lifted.

Inside `Game::Update` just add an else clause to the end of the conditional statement that checks if the player is alive, and call `ResetGame` if the action is triggered.

```
if (_player->GetIsAlive())
{
  // ...
}
else
{
  if (_tapAction->IsTriggered())
    ResetGame();
}
```

Now we can play the game, and if we collide with four enemies the game over screen will appear, displaying the score and allowing us to restart if we tap or click anywhere. We are now ready to add in the Live Tiles and sharing that was promised earlier.

Sharing in Windows 8

Social networks are incredibly popular, and sharing details about gameplay and high scores with friends is becoming a big feature of games, whether they're played on the web, on a tablet, or even on a console. More and more games have social integration of some sort and some console games allow you to tweet your game progress or status to friends, adding an extra level of immersion and integration with the real world. Windows 8 allows you to add that sharing easily, and gives the power to the players to decide when they want to share and how they want to share, using any of their favorite applications. This is called the **Share Charm**, and it is accessed via the charms bar on the right-hand side of the screen.

The Share Charm

There are two ways in which applications can interact with this system: as a **share source**, or as a **share target**. A share source just provides information to be shared on request to the operating system, while the share target receives the shared information and does what is necessary to complete the sharing operation. Games can take advantage of both sides where appropriate. In most cases a game will simply be a share source like ours will be; however, some games can benefit from receiving certain types of information. An example is a jigsaw game, which could let the player share an image from another application to use as a puzzle during a later game. This system facilitates the communication and provides a unique connection between otherwise unrelated applications and games.

To become a share source we need to do two things:

- Register for the `DataRequested` event
- Provide the information when that event fires

All of this operates through the `DataTransferManager` class, which is a WinRT type in charge of the share system. In our `Game` class we will register a handler named `ShareHandler` using the previously covered `TypedEventHandler` class.

```
DataTransferManager::GetForCurrentView()->DataRequested +=
  ref new
  Windows::Foundation::TypedEventHandler<
    DataTransferManager^,
    DataRequestedEventArgs^>(
      this,
      &Game::ShareHandler);
```

Once that is done we can implement the method, as shown in the following code snippet:

```
void Game::ShareHandler(
  DataTransferManager^ manager,
  DataRequestedEventArgs^ args)
{
  auto request = args->Request;

  if (!_player->GetIsAlive())
  {
    request->Data->Properties->Title =
      "My Score in Sample Game";
    request->Data->Properties->Description =
```

```
        "Check out my latest score in Sample Game!";
    request->Data->SetText(
        "I just scored " +
        _playerScore +
        " points in Sample Game!");
    }
    else
        request->FailWithDisplayText(
            "Cannot share until the game is over."
            );
    }
```

In this share handler we do two things: we first ensure that the player is only trying to share when the game is over, and we do this with a simple check to see if the player is alive. If not we use the request object to tell Windows that the operation should fail, and give a little hint as to why it did.

If we are on the Game Over screen, we fill in the **Title**, **Description**, and **Content** of the request with appropriate data that will be interpreted as required by the destination application. We simply set the relevant properties, and call SetText on the Data property to specify we are sharing text. If we have other types of data to share we can specify that as well. Once that is done we just return from the method and Windows takes it from there.

> If you want to generate the shared data asynchronously, you need to request a deferral using request->GetDeferral(). For more information on this, visit http://msdn.microsoft.com/en-us/library/windows/apps/windows.applicationmodel.datatransfer.datarequestdeferral.aspx.

The chosen application will then be invoked and notified that the user wants to share data with it. The application can then retrieve the data and do whatever it needs to do to share the data.

To try this out, play the game and collide with enough enemies to trigger the game over screen. While that is visible move your mouse to the top-right corner of the screen (or swipe in from the right on a touch device) and click on the **Share** button that appears. From there you can choose which application to share the information with, depending on what you have installed.

Sharing to the Mail App

WinRT components

Windows 8 provides a common API for applications developed in C++, C#, or Javascript to work with. It would be a lot of work to rewrite the API, or create wrapper APIs for each language, so instead of doing that the Windows team developed a system where a component written in one of the languages can be exposed to the other languages through a minimal translation layer. As developers, we can use this to access components written in other languages easily and with minimal performance impact. These components exist with DLLs that act in a manner similar to .NET class libraries; however, they can also be consumed by C++ and JavaScript.

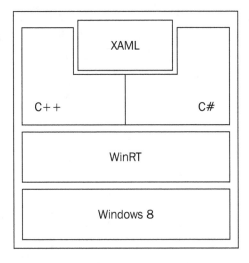

To create one of these, you simply create a **WinRT Component** project in Visual
Studio and write code using either C# or C++/CX. Only ref types in C++/CX will
be exposed to WinRT, so if you're writing a game or application in C# and want to
use a C++ only library, you can write a basic wrapper that includes native code in
your component, and expose that through ref classes and `Windows::Foundation`
namespace types for use in C# or JavaScript.

A wrapper is a simple method (or class) that exists to call another
function. It allows us to write code that connects systems together
where previously that might not have been possible. For example, a
WinRT component can act as a wrapper between (pure) native C/C++
code and managed code.

There are some restrictions when working with this system, because the component
must fit a lowest common denominator feature set for the available languages. In
this case many object-oriented features such as generics or runtime templates are
not available in JavaScript at all, and so those must be excluded from a WinRT type.
Classes exposed through WinRT must also be marked as sealed, as inheriting from a
WinRT type is not possible.

If you can work with the restrictions (which the compiler will happily outline), you
can gain great benefits from writing code in one language and using it in another.
As an example, we will write the live tile code in the next section in C# as a WinRT
component, and consume that code in our C++ game. To simplify the interface
between C# and C++ we'll handle the XML manipulation in C#; however, if you want
to stick with C++ for all of this you can utilize the same methods and functionality
within C++ (using C++/CX) and make use of your favorite XML parser.

You may be wondering how this fits into the traditional include filesystem used in C++, for components written in languages that do not require them.

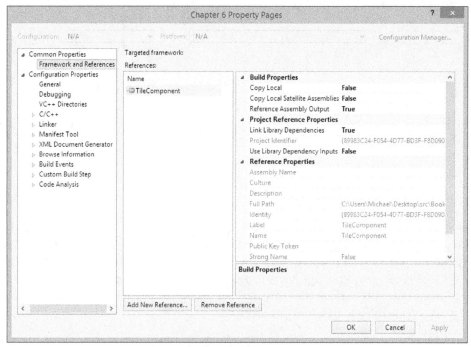

Framework and References dialog

By using the references dialog inside your project settings, you can add WinRT components and they will be implicitly included and recognized by the compiler.

Live tiles

Live tiles are a unique feature of the Windows platform. They allow developers to include information in the "icon" of the application. A great example would be an e-mail count indicator or a summary of the weather for the day. These tiles can update in the background even if the application is not running and provide a rich out of app experience.

Games can take advantage of this feature in any way they want, and some examples include showing a screenshot of a great achievement in the game, or showing the highest score the player has achieved. We will be using the live tile system to display the latest score of the player, and update it when the game ends. This way, players can show off their scores to their friends in person, and see how they did, which can lead to them playing the game even more because they don't need to enter the game to see their scores and get inspired to play.

There are two types of Live Tiles:

- **Application tiles** represent the main tile of the application. This is what you pin to the start menu and clicking on this will take you into the application as normal. On these tiles you would display the main information you want the user to see.

- **Secondary tiles** allow the application to provide shortcuts to different functionality within the application. For example, an email application may provide a Compose tile that exists as a shortcut to the compose screen within the application. Another example may be having separate tiles for different folders or email accounts. Each one can be a live tile and display information relevant to its own context, such as the unread count for the folder connected to the tile.

You can use either one, but secondary tiles must be created from within the application, while application tiles may be pinned by the user at any time, and are often auto-pinned when the application is installed.

As mentioned in the previous section, we will develop this in C# using a WinRT component, and then make use of it in our game using a single line of code.

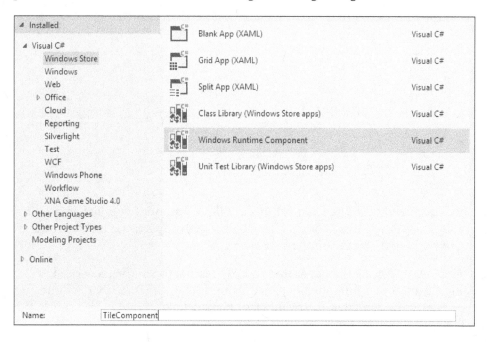

To begin, create a new Windows Runtime Component project in the same solution and name it TileComponent. Ensure you're looking at the Visual C# templates, and if you can't find the project type use the search box or filter using the **Windows Store** option.

Once this has been created, open the project properties for your C++ game, expand the **Common Properties** section in the side tree view, and select **Framework and References**.

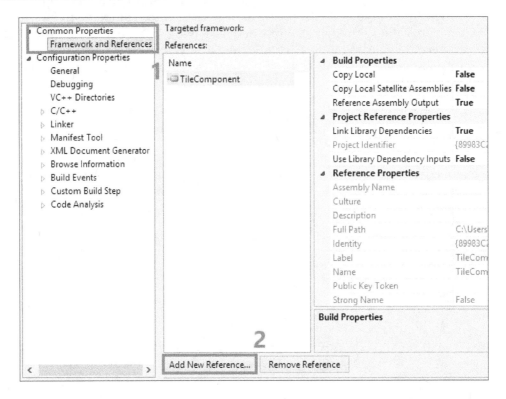

Click on **Add New Reference** and select the **TileComponent** you just created from the provided list. Once this is done, close the project properties window and look at the newly created **TileComponent** project.

We'll begin by renaming the generated Class1.cs file to TileManager.cs, accepting the offer to automatically rename the class itself. Once that is done, open up the file and you'll see a sealed class named TileManager. If you don't, make the appropriate edits.

We're going to add one method here to select the type of tile we want and set the data. Add in a new static method named `UpdateScoreTile`, which takes an integer parameter that we will name `score`.

```
public static void UpdateScoreTile(int score)
{
}
```

This will allow us to easily set the tile from our game using a single line of code.

Once that is done, we need to retrieve the template xml definition for the type of tile we want. There are many tile types available, and a full list can be found at `http://msdn.microsoft.com/en-us/library/windows/apps/hh761491.aspx`.

We do this with a call to `GetTemplateContent`, which is a static method sitting inside `Windows.UI.Notifications.TileUpdateManager`. This method takes an enumeration named `TileTemplateType`, which provides quick access to the many different tile types specified in the aforementioned link. In our case we want to use `TileSquareText01`, which provides us with a square tile that has a larger heading line, and then three text lines underneath. We will use these lines in the following manner:

1. Game name.

2. Score:.

3. The player's score.

This method will provide us with an XML object that we can manipulate to insert our desired values, which we will then provide to the update method that will do the rest for us.

Here is an example of the template XML generated by `GetTemplateContent`:

```
<tile>
  <visual>
    <binding template="TileSquareText01">
      <text id="1">Text Field 1</text>
      <text id="2">Text Field 2</text>
      <text id="3">Text Field 3</text>
      <text id="4">Text Field 4</text>
    </binding>
  </visual>
</tile>
```

The template itself looks similar to the preceding block of XML. You can see there are four lines of text available (in the template they're empty). If you wanted to pre-define this XML and store it within your code, or in a separate file, you could do this, load it in, and avoid the manipulation we're doing. As we want to update part of the text based on the score, we're going to use the template and not worry about hand crafting the XML.

```
var textElements = xml.GetElementsByTagName("text");
textElements[0].InnerText = "Sample Game";
textElements[1].InnerText = "Score:";
textElements[2].InnerText = score.ToString();
```

Here you can see why we are using C# to manipulate the XML. We can easily set the different lines as required. As shown, each of the lines are **text** tags so we can easily retrieve those and set them in order. We begin with the name of the game, and then a literal string that will display `Score:` before setting the score as the third string. We can leave the fourth string as is, and it will not appear on the tile.

Once we have the XML ready, we just need to create a new `TileNotification` and apply our XML data to it. With that, we can create a tile updater for the application tile (as opposed to a secondary tile) and call `Update`, passing in the notification we provided, as shown:

```
var notification = new TileNotification(xml);
TileUpdateManager.CreateTileUpdaterForApplication().
Update(notification);
```

This is all we need on the C# side to update the tile. Now we just need to add the following line to the end of the `EndGame` method within our Game class:

```
TileComponent::TileManager::UpdateScoreTile(_playerScore);
```

As you can see, no effort is required to consume the WinRT component, and it can even be easier to use than a C++ class within the same project.

Remember that there are pros and cons to everything, and while there can be major productivity boosts to developing a component in another language or using existing code, there is still a small memory and performance penalty, especially if you are transitioning between managed and unmanaged code, as we are here. This performance penalty comes from the need to marshal the data types between native code (C++) and managed code (C#). The shift over to managed code also introduces the .NET garbage collector, which requires the runtime to start tracking the data.

While the impact is minimal, this could add up if you are doing it many times each frame. Also remember that because WinRT components need to support JavaScript, they apply restrictions that may make it difficult to create nicely designed code. Evaluate the need on a case by case basis and choose the best option for your situation. In our case we are calling this once when the game ends, presenting a negligible performance impact. If you want to use managed code in other areas of your game, it is recommended that you cache references to objects to reduce the impact of transitioning between native and managed code.

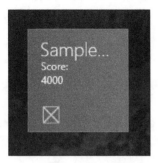

Now if you play the game and lose, not only can you share the score you've achieved, but you can also exit the game and see the tile update with your latest score. (Make sure you have pinned your game to the start menu to see this.)

Summary

So now we have a game with a lot more polish. It ends, and displays the final score to the user. It also takes advantage of unique Windows 8 features such as easy sharing with the Share Charm and Live Tiles, allowing you to display information to the user even when the game is not running.

There are many different ways to use these features depending on your game and situation. Remember that you want to ensure that you provide the best experience to your players if you want them to buy your games, and taking advantage of what the platform offers is a great way to do this.

We also looked at Windows Runtime (WinRT) components and saw how they can improve productivity by allowing you to develop in languages that have libraries or features that make certain tasks much easier. If you can afford the tiny performance impact then you should take advantage of this great Windows 8 feature in your game development and use it to make your development experience even better.

Next steps

Now that we have the game in place, we aren't far from placing this in the store and selling it to gamers around the world. Another feature found in many games is multiplayer, and in the next chapter we will take a look at how you can add this to your game using the networking functionality provided by Windows 8. We'll look at how to add a simple co-operative mode to the game so that a friend can play along or compete for score in real time. To do this we'll take a look at the different systems available to discover new games, how to communicate between two devices, and how to glue it all together with the menu system promised at the start of this chapter.

7
Playing Games with Friends

One of the biggest features in modern games is multiplayer, either over the internet or on a local network. Xbox Live, for example, is one of the largest multiplayer networks, and games such as Halo and Battlefield have incredible communities that sometimes never even play the single player component of the game. For this reason, multiplayer is a valid and powerful concept that should be considered for your games, although it may not always be appropriate for what you are creating. If your game doesn't fit a competitive mode of multiplayer, consider a cooperative mode. If multiplayer doesn't feel like it matches the experience that you want to provide, leave it out. The important thing is to ensure you focus on ensuring quality and fun, rather than adding in features that might not work.

One thing that I've omitted so far is a user interface system. This is crucial to multiplayer gaming as you need a way for the user to choose the multiplayer option and then receive information about who they are connecting to and even the status of the connection. For this reason, I'm going to explain a simple user interface system and how to go about implementing it so that you'll be able to if you want to add polish to your game, and even add a multiplayer mode.

After that small diversion, we'll look at what goes into multiplayer in modern games and your options for implementing that on Windows 8. You'll get an idea of how to make a connection to another machine and how to communicate data using the newly-styled Socket APIs and **DataReader/DataWriter**.

Later in this chapter you will have:

- Learned about the Proximity API and game discovery
- Looked at the topology of networked games
- Learned about sockets and how to use them
- Learned how to implement a user interface
- Learned how to communicate between different machines

A better menu system

In this section we will look at the changes that need to be made to move from basic text support to a slightly more advanced user interface system that we will need for the game, as well as the basic setup so we can focus on networking later on. If you want to jump to the networking part of this chapter, feel free to skip this section. Here we'll look at one kind of implementation that you could use.

Right now we just have a way to display text using some `TextBlock` objects that we can add to the renderer; however, even just switching between the score display and the game over message requires a bit of coding work to remove and add the text blocks one-by-one, as well as store their state individually. To get around this we're going to create a menu object that can store the state of the menu and allow us to easily construct and change menus. For the purposes of the sample we only need text functionality; however, this can also let you display textures for the different UI elements, allowing you to create a richer user interface.

For this system we have three classes: `Menu`, `ControlBase`, and `TextBlock` (inside `Menu.h`, `ControlBase.h`, and `TextBlock.h`). The `ControlBase` is an abstract class with the following definition:

```
enum class FocusState
{
  Unfocused,
  Focused
};

class ControlBase abstract
{
protected:
  bool _isVisible;
  DirectX::XMFLOAT2 _pos;
  Placement _placement;
  bool _canFocus;

public:
  virtual void Draw(std::shared_ptr<SpriteBatch> spriteBatch,
FocusState focused) = 0;
  virtual void HandleClick() = 0;
  virtual bool PointInBounds(float x, float y) = 0;

  void SetVisibility(bool value) { _isVisible = value; };
  bool GetVisibility() { return _isVisible; };

  void SetPlacement(Placement p) { _placement = p; };
```

```
Placement GetPlacement() { return _placement; };

void SetPosition(DirectX::XMFLOAT2 pos) { _pos = pos; };
void SetPosition(float x, float y) { SetPosition(DirectX::XMFLOAT2
(x, y)); };
DirectX::XMFLOAT2 GetPosition() { return _pos; };

void SetCanFocus(bool canFocus) { _canFocus = canFocus; };
bool GetCanFocus() { return _canFocus; };
};
```

For reference, `Placement` is an enumeration that we will use to position the origin of the control, allowing for easier layout. We will only implement support for `TopLeft` and `Center` origins; however, if you want to support other locations, just add in support to the drawing methods in your inheriting controls, as follows:

```
enum class Placement
{
  Place_TopLeft,
  Place_Center
};
```

Most of the methods in `ControlBase` are standard object-oriented ways to access the private variables, the main ones we need to consider are `Draw()`, `HandleClick()`, and `PointInBounds()`. These methods will be implemented in the subclass that inherits from `ControlBase`; however, `HandleClick` and `PointInBounds` are used by the `Menu` class to allow for interaction with the control. We'll look at how to implement these when we look at the `TextBlock` class.

Once you have this in place, we can implement the `Menu` class, which will handle storing the controls as well as managing which control is in focus and which control the mouse or finger is touching, as shown in the code snippet that follows:

```
class Menu
{
private:
  std::vector<std::shared_ptr<ControlBase>> _controls;
  std::shared_ptr<ControlBase> _focusControl;

public:
  Menu(void);
  ~Menu(void);

  void Draw(std::shared_ptr<SpriteBatch> spriteBatch);
  void ProcessClick(float x, float y);
```

```
   void ProcessClick();

   void AddControl(std::shared_ptr<ControlBase> control);
   bool SetFocus(std::shared_ptr<ControlBase> control = nullptr);
   void NextFocus();
};
```

The menu stores all of the controls, and tracks which one has focus for alternative input methods such as the controller. The `Draw()` method simply loops through the controls and draws them if their `Visibility` flag is set to `true`. The interesting methods are `ProcessClick()` and the two focus methods.

`ProcessClick()` manages the hit detection and messaging for the user interface. The x and y position values of the mouse or touch point are passed to the menu when the external code (in this case, the `Game` class) detects a click or tap. The `ProcessClick()` method without parameters exists to allow for gamepad interaction with the controls by clicking on the currently focused control instead of trying to detect the control based on the mouse position.

This brings us to the focus methods. These allow the menu to track the currently focused control, and also cycle through all of the controls that can be focused on (because you don't want to focus on the information text).

This menu is a bare bones implementation for this example; however, there are many different ways to handle user interfaces in games. With Windows 8 you can even choose to use **XAML** for your interface, and render over your game. If you haven't encountered it before, XAML stands for **Extensible Application Markup Language**, and refers to the XML-like language that can be used to define the look of a user interface. Although outside of the scope of this book, this system can be used with your DirectX game to handle the user interface (it uses DirectX to render itself) and, using C++/CX or the WinRT component system mentioned previously, you can connect the two together to create a complete system. If you find that you need more than the basic UI functionality outlined here, you may want to consider using XAML to handle it for you.

The implementation for the `Menu` class is as shown in the following code snippet:

```
void Menu::Draw(std::shared_ptr<SpriteBatch> spriteBatch)
{
  for (auto c : _controls)
  {
    if (c->GetVisibility())
      c->Draw(spriteBatch, c == _focusControl);
  }
}
```

The `Draw()` method simply draws the controls by iterating through the list and calling the control's `Draw()` method if it is visible, as can be seen in the code snippet that follows:

```
void Menu::AddControl(std::shared_ptr<ControlBase> control)
{
  _controls.push_back(control);
}

void Menu::ProcessClick(float x, float y)
{
  for (auto item : _controls)
  {
    if (item->GetVisibility() && item->PointInBounds(x, y))
    {
      item->HandleClick();
      break;
    }
  }
}

void Menu::ProcessClick()
{
  if (_focusControl != nullptr)
    _focusControl->HandleClick();
}
```

The `AddControl()` method is straightforward; we simply add the control to the list. `ProcessClick()` is the method that handles determining which control the user has clicked on, so that the associated logic can be executed. We provide two overloads for the `ProcessClick()` method so that we can simulate a click with the gamepad instead of choosing the focused control as the target for the click.

As shown in the following code snippet, the `SetFocus()` and `NextFocus()` methods both coordinate the control that is currently focused within the `Menu` class:

```
bool Menu::SetFocus(std::shared_ptr<ControlBase> control)
{
  if (control == nullptr || control->GetCanFocus())
  {
    _focusControl = control;
    return true;
  }
  else
    return false;
```

```
    }

    void Menu::NextFocus()
    {
      if (_focusControl == nullptr)
        _focusControl = _controls.at(0);
      else
      {
        auto it = _controls.begin();
        for (; it != _controls.end(); ++it)
        {
          if (*it == _focusControl)
          {
            ++it;
            break;
          }
        }
        if (it != _controls.end())
          _focusControl = *it;
        else
          _focusControl = nullptr;
      }
    }
```

SetFocus() allows us to explicitly set a particular control as the focused control, while NextFocus() iterates through the control list until it finds the currently focused control, and then proceeds through the list until it finds another control that can be focused on. This new control becomes the focused control at this point.

Now let's take a look at the implementation of the TextBlock class:

```
class TextBlock :
  public ControlBase
{
private:
  std::wstring _text;
  std::shared_ptr<SpriteFont> _font;
  DirectX::XMVECTOR _color, _focusCol;
  std::function<void (TextBlock*)> _clickHandler;

public:
  TextBlock(std::wstring fontPath);
  ~TextBlock(void);

  void SetText(std::wstring &text) { _text = text; };
```

```
    std::wstring& GetText() { return _text; };

    virtual void Draw(std::shared_ptr<SpriteBatch> sb, FocusState
focused);
    virtual void HandleClick();
    virtual bool PointInBounds(float x, float y);

    void MeasureString(std::wstring &str, int *width, int *height);
    void MeasureString(int *width, int *height);

    void SetColor(DirectX::FXMVECTOR color) { _color = color; };
    void SetFocusColor(DirectX::FXMVECTOR color) { _focusCol = color; };

    void SetClickHandler(std::function<void (TextBlock*)> func) { _
clickHandler = func; };

    static std::shared_ptr<TextBlock> Create(const wchar_t *font, const
wchar_t *text, float x, float y, Placement placement);
};
```

Here you can see that we have implemented the pure virtual methods in
`ControlBase`, as well as some get/set methods for the text and color variables.
Another method of note here is the `MeasureString()` method, which has the
same implementation that we had earlier. We also have a helper that sets common
parameters, such as the position and placement, to make our creation code cleaner.

Finally we used the `std::function` class to allow for a function to be stored so
that it can be called when the control is clicked on. With this we can use lambdas or
normal functions to implement code that will run when the control is clicked on, and
the `std::function` (inside `<functional>`) makes adding this in easy.

```
void TextBlock::HandleClick()
{
  if (_clickHandler != nullptr)
    _clickHandler(this);
}
```

We allow for external code to run if the `TextBlock` is clicked on, so we need a nice
way to trigger this code. For this we just ensure that an external method has actually
been associated with `_clickHandler`, and then if one has been associated we can call
that method.

```
void TextBlock::Draw(std::shared_ptr<SpriteBatch> sb, bool focused)
{
  if (_text.empty()) return;

  // Calculate position
```

```
          DirectX::XMFLOAT2 origin = DirectX::XMFLOAT2(0, 0);

          if (_placement == Placement::Place_Center)
          {
            int w, h;
            MeasureString(&w, &h);
            origin.x = w / 2.0f;
            origin.y = h / 2.0f;
          }

          _font->DrawString(
            sb.get(),
            _text.data(),
            _pos,
            (focused && _canFocus) ? _focusCol : _color,
            0.0F,
            origin);
        }
```

To draw the `TextBlock` we first need to make sure that there is text to render; otherwise, we shouldn't bother. If there is, then we need to determine the origin point of the text, which will allow us to implement our `Placement` functionality. In the case of `Place_TopLeft`, we just stick with an origin of `(0, 0)`. The difference comes when we handle `Placement::Place_Center`, which requires us to find the middle of the `TextBlock` by measuring the string with our `SpriteFont`. Finally we draw the string using the `DrawString()` method provided by our `SpriteFont`. At this point we also check if the control is focused, so that we can apply the alternate focus color if it is.

Let's finish up by digging deeper into the implementation of the `PointInBounds()` method:

```
        bool TextBlock::PointInBounds(float x, float y)
        {
          int width, height;
          MeasureString(&width, &height);
          float hw = (float)width / 2.0f;
          float hh = (float)height / 2.0f;
          float x1, x2;
          float y1, y2;
          switch (_placement)
          {
          case Placement::Place_Center:
            x1 = _pos.x - hw;
            x2 = x1 + (float)width;
            y1 = _pos.y - hh;
```

```
      y2 = y1 + (float)height;
      break;

   case Placement::Place_TopLeft:
      x1 = _pos.x;
      x2 = x1 + (float)width;
      y1 = _pos.y;
      y2 = y1 + (float)height;
      break;
   }

   return (x >= x1) && (x <= x2) && (y >= y1) && (y <= y2);
}
```

The actual check to see if the point is within the bounds of the control is in the last line of the code; however, we first need to get the bounds of the control. We will do this by determining the size of the string using our MeasureString() function, and then adjust those against the position, which itself is adjusted based on the placement of the origin of the control.

Now you can make use of the TextBlock::Create, Menu::AddControl() and TextBlock::SetClickHandler() methods to put together a menu or interface for your game.

If you haven't seen the changes in C++11 before, you might not know about lambdas and how they can improve your code. The following is an example of a lambda statement:

```
spButton->SetClickHandler(
[this] (TextBlock *s)
{
   StartGame(Mode_Singleplayer);
});
```

Here we're setting the click handler for the Singleplayer button, and inside that we're using something called a lambda, which is a new language feature that effectively allows us to define a function within another function, and use it as an object. There are three parts to the lambda here. The first part, [this] is the capture section. Here you can specify objects (pointers or references) within the containing function's scope that will be made available to the lambda. We provide the [this] pointer so that we can call the StartGame() method from within the lambda. (TextBlock *s) represents the parameter block for the lambda function, and in this case we need to match the method signature that the SetClickHandler() method expects, which is just a TextBlock parameter. Finally, we have the function body inside the opening and closing braces.

Think about what you might need to do to integrate menus with the sample game, or what other classes you could add. Remember that the less you write the better, and if a text block handles your needs for input, you don't necessarily need a button, as shown earlier. If you wanted a texture for a button, how might you go about adding support for that using what you have learned in this book?

Now let's move on to the real focus of this chapter: networking, and how you can use features and APIs in Windows 8 to add support for this feature.

Networking

There are two stages to a networked game: the game creation/joining stage, and the gameplay stage. As is the norm with game development, there are many different ways to approach and design these stages, and you should choose the right one (or combination) based on the needs of your game.

In this section we will look at the options available and where you might use each one, before looking at what Windows 8 provides and how to implement them.

For a long time, multiplayer gaming has been an important part of many games, and sometimes it is the primary part of the game, getting a much larger focus than the finely-crafted single player experiences on offer. Games from the Battlefield and Call of Duty series, for example, place a high importance on multiplayer gaming, and many fans buy the game just to play with others, some not even touching the single player experience. While this may seem like the easy way to avoid writing intelligent opponents for single player, multiplayer can often be incredibly difficult to get right, as the players will complain if there are issues, and will often break your game in ways you never even thought of. Also, if you create a single player game, and then decide you want to add in multiplayer, you will find that it is often very difficult to adapt the engine to the new style of play. For these reasons, you should consider multiplayer to be a primary experience for your game if you plan to include it, and devote a good amount of time to getting it right if you want to keep your players happy.

Choosing between client/server and peer-to-peer models

One of the first decisions you may face is choosing whether you want to go with the traditional **client/server** model, or the **peer-to-peer** model for game communication.

The client/server model

The client/server model treats one machine as the server, just like a web server, and this machine acts as the central authority for the game. All other players connect to this server and receive their updates from that one location. There are a few benefits to this, including being able to dedicate a machine as a server without a player, and providing extra resources to allow more players to join. Additionally, by adopting this model you can treat your entire game as a client/server multiplayer game, even if the player is running the single player aspect of your game. The Source engine (Half-Life 2, Team Fortress 2) does this using a concept called a **listen server**. This server runs privately on the local machine, and the game client connects to it to play the game. Of course, here you have the benefit of being able to separate out your game logic from your display and audio logic, which allows you to easily swap out the game for another with minimal effort by writing some new server logic.

Furthermore, cheat prevention can be implemented by checking the updates sent to the server and ensuring that the game state remains clean. If the values seem wrong or information from the client seems unusual, you can let the server fix the world state or remove the player.

There are downsides to this method, however. As there is a single point of contact for all players in a game, if this server goes offline or has an error, all players in the game will lose their connections and have to stop playing. The real-time nature of most video games makes traditional failover techniques unfeasible as the overhead to keep multiple backup servers in sync can often be too high. This, of course, depends on the game; for example, **Massively Multiplayer Online Games** (MMOG/MMO) are designed to run persistent worlds, and often utilize gameplay or world-building techniques that allow for backup servers to be kept in sync and in use through slower gameplay.

The peer-to-peer model

Another technique is the peer-to-peer model, or **P2P** for short. This model does away with the host/client relationship and instead connects each player to every other player, sharing the game data with everyone else and making decisions on local machines. This has numerous benefits, the most notable being the ability to handle loss of connection for any player and still keep the game going. In this case, the world state is communicated to every other player and each game client is responsible for both the rendering side of the game and the gameplay logic and state.

In this case you can set up a quick game with friends without the need to sort out an official server to host your game. **Matchmaking**, a technique where players are matched together without all agreeing to connect to a server is often used here as it allows for a master server to join everyone together, and then the peer-to-peer networking takes care of the rest. Data use is also spread among the players and, although each machine has to send out data to every other player, techniques can be used to minimize this and only send out the minimal amount, removing the bottleneck of having all the data have to arrive at a single point and leave from a single point. One example is to have all the players maintain a copy of the game state, and only the basic changes need be communicated across, rather than the state of the entire game world. Each client sends data about its own player to everyone else, ultimately reducing the amount of data travelling around.

There are negatives here as well. One popular aspect of online first person shooters is the **dedicated server**, which can then be connected to at any time. Want to jump on and practice against random people on the internet? Just jump online. However, with a peer-to-peer setup you need to use a matchmaking service to set this up. If you want to allow the players to remain together, you need to consider implementing group functionality to ensure that the players always join the same games.

Maybe a hybrid?

But what about taking the best of both worlds to try and get all of the benefits? Some developers make use of a hosted peer-to-peer model, where the players connect in a P2P fashion, and then the game decides on a host who will run the game. If that host has connection difficulties and drops out of the game, a new host will be selected, creating a momentary disruption to gameplay; however, the game will still continue. This is known as **host migration**. Although not perfect, this is an interesting model because it allows for a central authority alongside the disconnections and ad hoc style of games that you have often seen on home consoles. This model will generate more traffic than a peer-to-peer model; however, it can be quite useful to have a central authority that can decide if player A actually hit player B.

The first stage

What about the other stage of networked games that we mentioned? The game creation and joining stage is where players will set up a game or seek out others to play against. For some games this may not exist; however, for most this will be the first stop for players before they can enter the game itself and start playing. As usual there are different ways to accomplish this, and your options may vary depending on what resources you have available both on the device being used and externally.

Most PC games with a client/server model utilize a **server list** system. In this setup, all game servers register with a master server that acts as a catalog for ongoing games. When people want to play, they consult the master server for all of the games they can join and proceed to select one from that list. The master server itself doesn't handle any gameplay duties; instead the clients connect directly to the host using the information provided by the master server.

In some cases you may not have an internet connection, so what do you do then? Depending on the system the game is running on, you have different options. If you are running on a local network, you can broadcast messages over the network asking for the other clients to respond. Alternatively, the game can ask the player to enter the IP address or computer name of the host and try to connect directly. Some systems even provide ways to connect using **infrared** or **Bluetooth**, allowing the operating system to handle the device connection for the game. Windows 8 offers a version of the latter option using the **PeerFinder** and **Proximity APIs**. Using these APIs, Windows 8 games can find nearby Bluetooth or **Wi-Fi Direct** devices running the game and connect at the request of the player.

 Wi-Fi Direct is a technology that allows devices to connect using Wi-Fi without requiring an access point. This means that devices can connect directly to each other in a manner similar to Bluetooth, while taking advantage of the high speeds of modern Wi-Fi.

Tap technologies allow players with compatible devices to just tap their devices together and set up a game with even less effort by using the Proximity API in Windows 8. If you're looking to set up a master server to handle this, you can easily use HTTP, with a web server and database on the other end.

The other thing you need to consider in this stage is the experience. Do you want the player to be able to join games in progress? How does this impact the gameplay stage? One commonly used option is the **game lobby**. This applies to both the client/server and peer-to-peer games, where the players can only join a game at the start of the match and for a period of time they sit in a lobby where they can chat while they wait. This is useful for a number of reasons. Players can start to join as soon as the game is created, even before the host has finished configuring the game parameters (often seen in RTS games), or maybe the game needs some more players and is actively searching (as is the case with matchmaking systems), and so players can sit and talk while the other players are found.

Whatever you choose, remember that they are there to play and you want to minimize their downtime as much as possible. If they're sitting forever in lobbies then they won't find the game fun and will quit playing. The best option is a game that allows players to drop in at any time; however, this isn't always possible and you need to choose what is right for your game.

Using the PeerFinder

One option on Windows 8 for connecting, if you don't want to set up a master server or UI for entering an IP address, is to use the PeerFinder API. This uses Wi-Fi and Bluetooth to find nearby machines to connect to and allows you to advertise and establish a connection with a few simple calls.

PeerFinder itself is part of the Proximity APIs, which also includes the ability to establish connections or open applications using the **Near Field Communication (NFC)** sensor that may be present in some devices.

 Proximity is a new API in Windows 8 that allows for easy operation and connection of devices that are physically close to each other. The focus of this API is to enable scenarios where two devices can easily connect and communicate using Bluetooth, NFC, or Wi-Fi Direct. By having a consolidated API, developers don't need to put a lot of effort into supporting the different communication types.

To begin working with PeerFinder, we need to start advertising that we are accepting connections. This is done with the `PeerFinder::Start()` static method. This call is also required if you want to search and connect to another peer, so you could enable a peer-to-peer situation where the game automatically starts advertising and then the players can decide who connects. This is shown in the code snippet that follows:

```
PeerFinder::Start();
PeerFinder::ConnectionRequested += ref new TypedEventHandler<Object^,
Windows::Networking::Proximity::ConnectionRequestedEventArgs^>(this,
&MyClass::HandleConnection);
```

To accept a connection we need to hook into the `ConnectionRequested` event, which will provide us with a `PeerInformation` object describing the peer that wants to connect. Using this we can call the `ConnectAsync()` method and accept the connection, which will provide us with a `StreamSocket` just like when you connect as a client. I'll describe how to work with this method in the following section.

The other scenario that `PeerFinder` supports is discovering and connecting to peers (as opposed to just advertising). How you present this to the player is up to you; however, by calling the `PeerFinder::Start()` method you begin advertising your machine as a peer, and others may try to connect to you. As `PeerFinder` only works when players are physically close to each other, you could safely implement this system as a local lobby where all the players can see each other, and then attempt to establish and accept each other's connections to start a game.

The first step to connect to someone else is to find the nearby peers, this is done with the `PeerFinder::FindAllPeersAsync()` method, as shown:

```
using namespace concurrency;

PeerFinder::Start();
auto op = PeerFinder::FindAllPeersAsync();
task<IVectorView<PeerInformation^>^> findAllPeersTask(op);
findAllPeersTask.then(
[this]
(concurrency::task<IVectorView<PeerInformation^>^> resultTask)
{
        auto peerList = resultTask.get();
});
```

The `Async` part of the `FindAllPeersAsync()` method indicates that this method will run in the background and eventually return the information we asked for, so we need to make use of the task system in WinRT to **continue** once the method completes.

 For more information on what Async is, refer to the *Side note – Async* section.

Once we retrieve the result, we have a list of peers available to work with. From there we need to convey this to the players so that they can select who they want to connect to. Meanwhile you need to store the `PeerInformation` objects stored in the list so that you can make use of them later. If you need an identifier to convey which connection is which to the players, you can use the `DisplayName` property, which will show the name of the machine detected.

Now that you have a `PeerInformation` object to connect to, you can call the `PeerFinder::ConnectAsync()` method, passing in the `PeerInformation` object to establish the connection, as shown:

```
auto op = PeerFinder::ConnectAsync(peer);
concurrency::task<StreamSocket^> connectTask(op);
connectTask.then(
[this](concurrency::task<StreamSocket^> resultTask)
{
    auto socket = resultTask.get();
    // Use socket to communicate
});
```

Once we continue after connecting, we can retrieve the `StreamSocket` and begin communicating.

Place a try/catch block around the `resultTask.get()` method to catch any exceptions that may occur. Windows will throw an exception if the connection fails, and this is where it will surface.

Communicating the gameplay

Once the player is in the game, we need to communicate the game state to the other players or the server. The communication of this data is done with a technology called **Sockets**. In Windows 8 there are two different types of sockets that define the protocol type that is used. We'll start by looking at the different options and how to get started with them before looking at how to read and write data using the `DataReader` and `DataWriter` classes.

TCP – StreamSocket

The standard option and the one provided when using the `PeerFinder` class in Windows 8 is the `StreamSocket`. This is a standard socket that creates a TCP connection between the host and client. There are benefits to this option; however, depending on how much data is sent back and forth, or how important you consider latency, you may want to choose the **User Datagram Protocol (UDP)** instead.

The **TCP** protocol establishes a connection between a host and client machine to communicate, and provides one major benefit: reliability. Any messages sent over a TCP connection have a reasonable guarantee that they will reach their destination, assuming there isn't any major fault or issue with the connection. This is accomplished by tracking the packets that are sent, and resending them as required to ensure the message arrives in order. That last part there has two important elements: the packets are resent, and they arrive in order. It wouldn't do to have important game information go missing (known as packet loss) without you knowing, or have the latter half of some game data arrive before the first half, without your knowledge. TCP takes away a lot of the worry when dealing with this as the operating system handles all of this for you.

These benefits come with a downside, though. There is an overhead associated with resending and reordering packets, which in the fast-paced game world can lead to issues in keeping two players in sync. If you aren't sending a lot of data then this isn't a big deal, and if your game doesn't require a new world state all the time then you could use this without worrying too much. If, however, you are writing a fast-paced game such as a first-person shooter that requires a constant stream of updates, you might want to consider using UDP instead.

To make use of this socket, you can either establish the connection yourself, or if you are using the `PeerFinder` class, the `ConnectAsync()` method will give you a connected `StreamSocket` that you can use in your game. Let's quickly take a look at how to create a `StreamSocket` manually.

There are two parts to a TCP connection: **listener** and **socket**. You should use the listener to wait and listen for an incoming connection, and then respond to that connection using a `StreamSocket`. This is defined in the following piece of code:

```
StreamSocketListener^ listener = ref new StreamSocketListener();
listener->ConnectionReceived += ref new TypedEventHandler<StreamSock
etListener^, StreamSocketListenerConnectionReceivedEventArgs^>(this,
&MyClass::HandleConnection);
listener->BindServiceNameAsync("6000");
```

For the server, we will start by creating a `StreamSocketListener`. This handles waiting for a connection and, if one occurs, the `ConnectionReceived` event is raised, which we hooked into earlier.

Once we have hooked into the `ConnectionReceived` event we can tell the listener to start listening, which we do using the `BindServiceNameAsync()` method. This method takes a string which in most cases will just specify a port number to listen on as shown earlier. Remember that this is the WinRT `Platform::String` rather than the standard library string, so ensure you're providing the correct one.

When a connection arrives, our handler will be called and we will be provided with a `StreamSocketListenerConnectionReceivedEventArgs` object. Inside this object we have one property: `Socket`. This is our `StreamSocket` for the connection, which is ready for use.

If you're looking to connect as a client, you'll need to start with a `StreamSocket` and provide an endpoint to connect to, as shown in the code snippet that follows:

```
auto host = ref new HostName("localhost");
auto port = ref new String(L"6000");
auto socket = ref new StreamSocket();
socket->ConnectAsync(host, port, SocketProtectionLevel::PlainSocket);
```

For the endpoint we need to provide the host name of the machine (or the IP address) and the port. Once we have that we just need to create a new `StreamSocket` and call the `ConnectAsync()` method, passing in the host and port. The third parameter allows you to create an SSL connection; however, further setup is required on the listener for that, and you don't really need it to connect two computers to play a game, so we won't look further into it.

UDP – DatagramSocket

The **UDP** has traditionally been the go-to protocol for game developers, as it provides the most control and the most performance, at the cost of the nice benefits mentioned in the TCP section earlier. If you haven't encountered this one before, UDP is considered a **connectionless protocol** because it doesn't establish a dedicated connection like TCP. Instead, messages (called **datagrams**) are transmitted as required and received whole. That is, unless they don't arrive. One of the primary downsides to UDP is its unreliability, as packets can be lost, and UDP provides no guarantee or built-in support for confirmation. Alongside, packets may take different routes and arrive out of order, and the UDP doesn't assist here either. This means that you will need to handle all of this yourself, either by enduring the problem (and working around the packet loss), or writing your own integrity checks to ensure you're getting the information you need.

The benefits come from the lightweight nature of the protocol. As there is no connection, and packet or order validation, we get a very thin layer that runs as fast as possible, meaning it is great for the real-time nature games where packet loss may be tolerated as long as we get a faster system.

As we are just working with single messages, we don't need to establish a connection, and instead our server just listens for individual messages. To do this we need to create a `DatagramSocket`, as shown:

```
DatagramSocket^ listenSocket = ref new DatagramSocket();
listenSocket->MessageReceived += ref new TypedEventHandler<Da
    tagramSocket^, DatagramSocketMessageReceivedEventArgs^>(this,
    &MyClass::ReceiveMessage);
listenSocket->BindServiceNameAsync("6000");
```

You can see that this is similar to the `StreamSocketListener` from the TCP server. However, in this case the `DatagramSocket` handles everything. Here we will create the new socket, and then hook into the `MessageReceived` event. Once we've done that we can tell the socket to bind to a particular port and start listening for messages with the `BindServiceNameAsync()` method, which takes the name of the service (or port) just like the TCP.

Inside `ReceiveMessage` (the handler for `MessageReceived`), we are provided with the listening socket and a `DatagramSocketMessageReceivedEventArgs` object as the method arguments. Here we can access the message itself by retrieving the `DataReader` from the `DatagramSocketMessageReceivedEventArgs` using `args->GetDataReader()`.

To send a message we need the endpoint that we want to connect to, the port, and the data we want to send. This is shown in the following piece of code:

```
auto host = ref new HostName("localhost");
auto port = ref new Platform::String(L"6000");
DatagramSocket^ socket = ref new DatagramSocket();
socket->ConnectAsync(hostName, ServiceNameForConnect->Text);
```

Here we perform similar steps to the `StreamSocket`, by creating the socket and telling it where to connect to. The following line will create a `DataWriter` that can be used to send the message:

```
auto writer = ref new DataWriter(socket->OutputStream);
```

Reading and writing data

So we have a socket and we want to communicate using it. For this, we have two classes that make it easier for us to construct the byte stream that will be sent to the other machine: the `DataReader` and `DataWriter` classes. By using these classes you also don't need to worry about byte order in the data you send, or how the data type is formatted.

Side note – Async

Before we look at those two classes, though, we need to take a very quick look at the Async system in WinRT. Every API call that doesn't always return immediately (and has Async in the name) will run asynchronously. This is all managed by Windows, but you need to be able to handle it. A call to the `ConnectAsync()` method won't return a socket because it immediately returns, allowing you to continue working while the connection is established in the background. For this reason we need to use the continuation system provided through the task parallel library in Windows. With this, we can provide code that will continue after the task has finished, so we can easily write the code that should run later, and tack it onto the end; the scheduler will take care of the rest.

This is a great place to use the new lambda feature introduced in C++11. This feature, similar to lambdas or anonymous delegates in C#, allows you to write a function within a function, and treat it as an object that can be passed as a parameter. This lets us avoid creating single line functions for these continuations and cluttering up our class declaration.

Let's take a look at the `PeerFinder::ConnectAsync()` method as an example:

```
auto op = PeerFinder::ConnectAsync(peer);
concurrency::task<StreamSocket^> connectTask(op);
connectTask.then([this](concurrency::task<StreamSocket^> resultTask)
```

```
{
    auto socket = resultTask.get();
    // Use socket to communicate
}
```

In here the `ConnectAsync` method returns a token, which we can use to check if the task is done at any point in time. However, a nicer way to handle this is to schedule some code to run right after the connection is established (or fails). To do that, we need to use the `concurrency::task` class, which will let us call the `task.then()` method. As you can see in the sample earlier, the `then()` method takes a function pointer, which we define as a lambda in this case. However, if you prefer to define the function separately, you can pass a reference to the function using legacy C-style function pointers.

The function signature needs to take the previous task as a parameter, which we can use to get the returned value using the `task.get()` method. If any exceptions have occurred asynchronously, this is where they will be rethrown so you can handle them. An example of this might be a failure during the socket connection. An exception is thrown but because the code is running asynchronously and you haven't written the code that is running, you can't catch the exception. The operating system will aggregate any exceptions and throw them when you call the `get()` method, allowing you to handle them then.

The DataReader

So we have a `DataReader` and we're ready to start retrieving messages or information from the stream. `DataReader` allows us to get the information we need while handling the type conversion for us by allowing us to call a method corresponding to the data type. For example, if you want to read a 32-bit signed integer from the stream, you can call the `reader->ReadInt32()` method and get an `int` back.

Before we do any of that, though, we need to load the right amount of data from the stream. As you might have guessed, this needs to happen asynchronously, using the `LoadAsync()` method, as shown in the following code snippet:

```
auto loadTask = concurrency::task<unsigned int>(reader-
>LoadAsync(sizeof(int)));
loadTask.then([this] (concurrency::task<unsigned int> result)
{
    if (result.get() == sizeof(int))
    {
        dataFromStream = reader->ReadInt32();
    }
});
```

The result of the `LoadAsync()` method is the actual number of bytes read, which allows you to check if you have the right amount of data, or only some of it. In the case of the stream sockets, you may want to keep loading until you have all of the required bytes, as any call to a Read function will throw an exception if there isn't enough data in the reader.

Assuming everything is good, you can retrieve the data using the appropriate Read function and continue from there.

> You can load in a large block of data and then read parts of it out in sequence if desired. This would be the optimal way of doing so; however, you will need to adjust the behavior based on what you're actually reading in and how you have constructed the data on the other end of the connection.

The DataWriter

The counterpart to the `DataReader` is the `DataWriter`. This class handles converting your data into bytes and writing them to the stream. In most cases you'll create the `DataWriter` using an `IOutputStream` taken from one of your sockets, as shown:

```
auto writer = ref new DataWriter(socket->OutputStream);
```

Once you have the writer you can then use the appropriate Write command to convert your data to bytes and save it to an internal buffer.

> At this point, your data has not been transmitted yet. We need to call another asynchronous method later on to do this.

Sending the data in a batched block of bytes is better than sending out a couple of bytes at a time, so by using the `DataWriter` you're also optimizing your throughput by allowing it to handle batching for you. This is done as follows:

```
writer->WriteInt32(10); // int
writer->WriteSingle(5.4f); // float
writer->WriteByte('a'); // unsigned char
```

These are some examples of the available Write methods that you can use to send your data. Once you're done writing out your message, you need to just make one more method call to finish up, as shown in the following piece of code:

```
writer->StoreAsync();
```

This asynchronous method will take the buffer that you've built up and write it to the stream, which in turn will send the data out on the socket to the other endpoint.

At this point the data has been sent and the other side will receive it at some point. Remember that these are asynchronous methods, so you should be careful to not try and write out more data until the `StoreAsync()` method is complete. If you're sending data in each frame, then you might want to only call the `StoreAsync()` method once you're done writing out all data for the frame. In the end, though, you'll want to ensure that you have some kind of synchronization in place to ensure that the `StoreAsync()` method is complete before you try to write any more. The same goes for the `LoadAsync()` method; do not try to load while the reader is still loading a previous request.

You might wonder, well, why not make these synchronous? Well in our case, we want the game client to continue rendering and updating so that the player doesn't notice an issue even if something is slowing the transfer. We need to output a new frame every 16 to 33 milliseconds; so even if we don't transmit a new message every frame, we should still render as normal.

Summary

Over the course of this chapter we've looked at a couple of different topics, from Graphical User Interfaces (GUIs) to different types of multiplayer topologies and how to connect to other computers with Windows 8.

These may be random topics, but, they are all crucial to adding in networked multiplayer, and hopefully by reading through this topic you now understand some of the many different options available, so you can implement multiplayer if you feel it fits your game.

You may have noticed that in this chapter we didn't alter the sample game. This leads back to what I mentioned before. It's important that you add features that will enhance your game, and if that means leaving out multiplayer, then you should do so. In our case the game didn't quite work with a multiplayer mode, so we left it out. However, keep it in mind for any games you make in the future, as it can really add to the replay value of your game if it works.

We also looked at the different types of sockets you might want to use, and why (or why not). Remember that UDP will require more work on your part, but gives a large speed boost that could be useful. If you don't need that latency you can make do with TCP and gain the benefits of ordered messages and reliable transmission.

Next steps

So we're done with our sample game, all of the features are in, and now it's time to look at getting it out there to an audience. Over the next two chapters we're going to look at what you need to do so your fans can download your game, from submission to certification. We'll look at the tools available to make certification easier, tips and tricks to remember so you pass the first time, and how to work through the submission process so that you can actually get your game into the store. After that we'll look at ways to monetize your game so you can make a profit on your work. freemium games are big and you might want to try out that business model, so we'll take a look at in-app purchases and how to add them to your game so you can make money even after the player downloads the game. If you don't want to go down that path, you can always sell your game upfront using the store, and adding a trial version of your game has never been easier. We'll take a look at the trial game options available to you, and how to add a timed trial version without changing any of your code.

8
Getting into the Store

So now you have a game, polished and ready to distribute. The next step is to get it into a place where others can download it, or maybe even buy it. In Windows 8 this would be the Windows Store. Just like most other app stores out there, the Windows store has a certification process that must be passed, but think of it as a great way to check the quality of your code and maybe even get some free testing before reviewing players get their hands on your game.

This chapter will look at the process to go about submitting your game for certification and sale. We'll look at each step that applies to games and the common issues that lead to certification failure. If you're looking for information on selling your game, or other ways to monetize it, check out the next chapter as we'll take a look at ways to make money from your game, including using trial mode and in-app purchases.

So over the course of this chapter we'll look at the following:

- Getting a Windows Store account
- Creating your game/reserving a name
- Windows Application Certification Kit
- Creating packages for the store
- Screenshots and icons
- Game ratings
- Submitting to the store
- Common issues with certification

Hopefully this and the next chapter will help you get your games out into the marketplace and into player's hands. Who knows, you might even make some money with them.

Note that, as the store is a service run by Microsoft, it is subject to change at any time. While correct at the time of writing, some information in this chapter may be incorrect and outdated in future.

Getting into the store

This all starts by visiting `https://appdev.microsoft.com/StorePortals`, which will get you to the store dashboard that you use to submit and manage your applications. If you already have an account you'll just log in here and proceed. If not, we'll take a look at ways of getting it set up.

There are a couple of ways to get a store account, which you will need before you can submit any game or application to the store. There are also two different types of accounts:

- Individual accounts
- Company accounts

In most cases you will only need the first option. It's cheaper and easier to get, and you won't require the enterprise features provided by the company account for a game. For this reason we'll focus on the individual account.

To register you'll need a credit card for verification, even if you gain a free account another way. Just follow the registration instructions, pay the fee, and complete verification, after which you'll be ready to go.

Free accounts

Students and developers with **MSDN subscriptions** can access registration codes that waive the fee for a minimum of one year. If you meet either of these requirements you can gain a code using the following methods, and use that code during the registration process to set the fee to zero.

Students can access their free accounts using the **DreamSpark** service that Microsoft runs. To access this you need to create an account on `www.dreamspark.com`. From there follow the steps to verify your student status and visit `https://www.dreamspark.com/Student/Windows-Store-Access.aspx` to get your registration code.

If you have access to an MSDN subscription you can use this to gain a store account for free. Just log in to your account and in your account benefits overview you should be able to generate your registration code.

Submitting your game

So your game is polished and ready to go. What do you need to do to get it in the store?

First log in to the dashboard and select **Submit an App** from the menu on the left. Here you can see the steps required to submit the app. This may look like a lot to do, but don't worry. Most of these are very simple to resolve and can be done before you even start working on the game.

The first step is to choose a name for your game, and this can be done whenever you want. By reserving a name and creating the application entry you have a year to submit your application, giving you plenty of time to complete it. This is why it's a good idea to jump in and register your application once you have a name for it. If you change your mind later and want a different name you can always change it.

The next step is to choose how and where you will sell your game. There are a number of options here; however, we won't cover selling your game until the next chapter.

The other thing you need to choose here is the markets you want to sell your game in. This can be an area you need to be careful of, because the markets you choose here define the localization or content you need to watch for in your game. Certain markets are restrictive, and including content that isn't appropriate for a market you say you want to sell in can cause you to fail the certification process.

Once that is done you need to choose when you want to release your game—you can choose to release as soon as certification finishes or on a specific date, and then you choose the app category, which in this case will be **Games**. Don't forget to specify the genre of your game as the sub-category so players can find it.

The final option on the **Selling Details** page that applies to us is the **Hardware requirements** section. Here we define the DirectX feature-level required for the game, and the minimum RAM required to run it. This is important because the store can help ensure that players don't try to play your game on systems that cannot run it.

The next section allows you to define the in-app offers that will be made available to players. If you want more information on this then please read through *Chapter 9, Monetization*.

The **Age rating and rating certificates** section allows you to define the minimum age required to play the game, as well as submit official ratings certificates from ratings boards so that they may be displayed in the store to meet legal requirements. The latter part is optional in some cases, and may affect where you can submit your game depending on local laws.

Aside from official ratings, all applications and games submitted to the store require a voluntary rating, chosen from one of the following age options:

- **3+**
- **7+**
- **12+**
- **16+**
- **18+**

While all content is checked, the 7+ and 3+ ratings both have extra checks because of the extra requirements for those age ranges. The 3+ rating is especially restrictive as apps submitted with that age limit may not contain features that could connect to online services, collect personal information, or use the webcam or microphone. To play it safe it's recommended the 12+ rating is chosen, and if you're still uncertain, higher is safer.

GDF Certificates

The other entry required here if you have official ratings certificates is a **GDF** file. This is a **Game Definition File**, which defines the different ratings in a single location and provides the necessary information to display the rating and inform any parental settings. To do this you need to use the GDFMAKER.exe utility that ships with the Windows 8 SDK, and generate a GDF file that you can submit to the store. Alongside that you need to create a DLL containing that file (as a resource) without any entry point to include in the application package. For full details on how to create the GDF as well as the DLL, view the following MSDN article:

http://msdn.microsoft.com/en-us/library/windows/apps/hh465153.aspx

The final section before you need to submit your compiled application package is the cryptography declaration. For most games you should be able to declare that you aren't using any cryptography within the game and quickly move through this step. If you are using cryptography, including encrypting game saves or data files, you will need to declare that here and follow the instructions to either complete the step or provide an **Export Control Classification Number** (**ECCN**).

Now you need to upload the compiled app package before you can continue, so we'll take a look at what it takes to do that before you continue.

App packages

To submit your game to the store, you need to package it up in a format that makes it easy to upload, and easy for the store to distribute. This is done by compiling the application as an .appx file. But before that happens we need to ensure we have defined all of the required metadata, and fulfill the certification requirements, otherwise we'll be uploading a package only to fail soon after.

Part of this is done through the application manifest editor, which is accessible in Visual Studio by double-clicking on the **Package.appxmanifest** file in solution explorer.

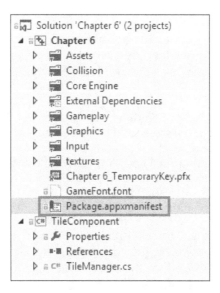

This editor is where you specify the name that will be seen in the start menu, as well as the icons used by the application. To pass certification all icons have to be provided at 100 percent DPI, which is referred to as **Scale 100** in the editor.

Icon/Image	Base resolution	Required
Standard	150 x 150 px	Yes
Wide	310 x 150 px	If Wide Tile Enabled
Small	30 x 30 px	Yes
Store	50 x 50 px	Yes
Badge	24 x 24 px	If Toasts Enabled
Splash	620 x 300 px	Yes

If you wish to provide a higher quality images for people running on high DPI setups, you can do so with a simple filename change. If you add `scale-XXX` to your filename, just before the extension, and replace XXX with one of the following values, Windows will automatically make use of it at the appropriate DPI.

- scale-100
- scale-140
- scale-180

In the following image you can see the options available for editing the visual assets in the application. These all apply to the start menu and application start-up experience, including the splash screen and toast notifications.

Toast Notifications in Windows 8 are pop-up notifications that slide in from the edge of the screen and show the users some information for a short period of time. They can click on the toast to open the application if they want. Alongside Live Tiles, Toast Notifications allow you to give the user information when the application is not running (although they work when the application is running).

The previous table shows the different images required for a Windows 8 application, and if they are mandatory or just required in certain situations. Note that this does not include the imagery required for the store, which includes some screenshots of the application and optional promotional art in case you want your application to be featured.

You must replace all of the required icons with your own. Automated checks during certification will detect the use of the default "box" icon shown in the previous screenshot and automatically fail the submission.

Capabilities

Once you have the visual aspects in place, you need to declare the capabilities that the application will receive. Your game may not need any, but you should still only specify what you need to run, as some of these capabilities come with extra implications and non-obvious requirements.

Adding a privacy policy

One of those requirements is the privacy policy. Even if you are creating a game, there may be situations where you are collecting private information, which requires you to have a privacy policy. The biggest issue here is connecting to the internet. If your game marks any of the Internet capabilities in the manifest, you automatically trigger a check for a privacy policy as private information—in this case an IP address—is being shared.

To avoid failing certification for this, you need to put together a privacy policy if you collect privacy information, or use any of the capabilities that would indicate you collect information. These include the Internet capabilities as well as location, webcam, and microphone capabilities. This privacy policy just needs to describe what you will do with the information, and directly mention your game and publisher name.

Once you have the policy written, it needs to be posted in two locations. The first is a publicly accessible website, which you will provide a link to when filling out the description after uploading your game. The second is within the game itself. It is recommended you place this policy in the Windows 8 provided settings menu, which you can build using XAML or your own code. If you're going with a completely native Windows 8 application you may want to display the policy in your own way and link to it from options within your game.

Declarations

Once you've indicated the capabilities you want, you need to declare any operating system integration you've done. For most games you won't use this, but if you're taking advantage of Windows 8 features such as share targets (the destination for data shared using the Share Charm), or you have a Game Definition File, you will need to declare it here and provide the required information for the operating system. In the case of the GDF, you need to provide the file so that the parental controls system can make use of the ratings to appropriately control access.

Certification kit

The next step is to make sure you aren't going to fail the automated tests during certification. Microsoft provides the same automated tests used when you submit your app in the **Windows Application Certification Kit (WACK)**.

 WACK is installed by default with Visual Studio 2012 or higher version.

There are two ways to run the test: after you build your application package, or by running the kit directly against an installed app. We'll look at the latter first, as you might want to run the test on your deployed test game well before you build anything for the store. This is also the only way to run the WACK on a WinRT device, if you want to cover all bases.

If you haven't already deployed or tested your app, deploy it using the **Build** menu in Visual Studio and then search for the Windows App Cert Kit using the start menu (just start typing). When you run this you will be given an option to choose which type of application you want to validate. In this case we want to select the Windows Store App option, which will then give you access to the list of apps installed on your machine. From there it's just a matter of selecting the app you want and starting the test. At this point you will want to leave your machine alone until the automated tests are complete. Any interference could lead to an incorrect failure of the certification tests.

The results will indicate ways you can fix any issues; however, you should be fine for most of the tests. The biggest issues will arise from third party libraries that haven't been developed or ported to Windows 8. In this case the only option is to fix them yourself (if they're open source) or find an alternative.

Once you have the test passing, or you feel confident that it won't be an issue, you need to create app packages that are compatible with the store. At this point your game will be associated with the submission you have created in the Windows Store dashboard so that it is prepared for upload.

Creating your app packages

To do this, right click on your game project in Visual Studio and click on **Create App Packages** inside the **Store** menu.

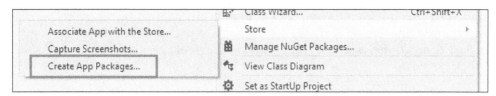

Once you do that, you'll be asked if you want to create a package for the store. The difference between the two options comes down to how the package is signed. If you choose **No** here, you can create a package with your test certificate, which can be distributed for testing. These packages must be manually installed and cannot be submitted to the store. You can, however, use this type of package on other machines to install your game for testers to try out. Choosing **No** will give you a folder with a .ps1 file (Powershell), which you can run to execute the install script.

Choosing **Yes** at this option will take you to a login screen where you can enter your Windows Store developer account details. Once you've logged in you will be presented with a list of applications that you have registered with the store.

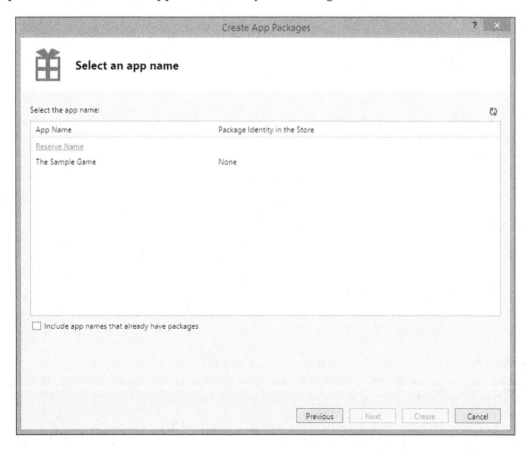

If you haven't yet reserved the name of your application, you can click on the **Reserve Name** link, which will take you directly to the appropriate page in the store dashboard. Otherwise select the name of the game you're trying to build and click on **Next**.

The next screen will allow you to specify which architectures to build for, and the version number of the built package. As this is a C++ game, we need to provide separate packages for the ARM, x86, and x64 builds, depending on what you want to support. Simply providing an x86 and ARM build will cover the entire market; 64 bit can be nice to have if you need a lot of memory, but ultimately it is optional, and some users may not even be able to run x64 code.

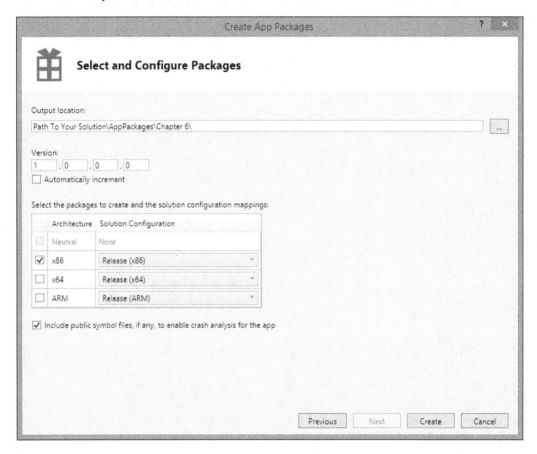

When you're ready click on **Create** and Visual Studio will proceed to build your game and compile the requested packages, placing them in the directory specified. If you've built for the store, you will need the .appxupload files from this directory when you proceed to upload your game.

Once the build has completed you will be asked if you want to launch the Windows Application Certification Kit. As mentioned previously this will test your game for certification failures, and if you're submitting to the store it's strongly recommended you run this. Doing so at this screen will automatically deploy the built package and run the test, so ensure you have a little bit of time to let it run.

Uploading and submitting

Now that you have a built app package you can return to the store dashboard to submit your game. Just edit the submission you made previously and enter the **Packages** section, which will take you to the page where you can upload the `appxupload` file.

Once you have successfully uploaded your game you will gain access to the next section, the **Description**. This is where you define the details that will be displayed in the store. This is also where your marketing skills come into play as you prepare the content that will hopefully get players to buy your game.

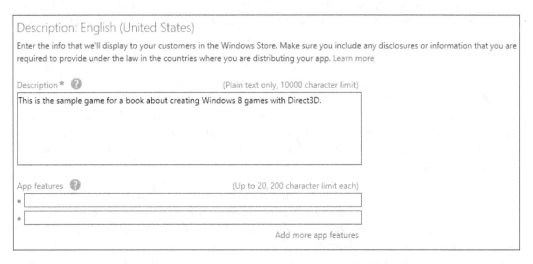

You start with the description of your game, and any big feature bullet points you want to emphasize. This is the best place to mention any reviews or praise, as well as give a quick description that will help the players decide if they want to try your game. You can have a number of app features listed; however, like any "back of the box" bullet points, keep them short and exciting.

Along with the description, the store requires at least one screenshot to display to the potential player. These screenshots need to be of the entire screen, and that means they need to be at least **1366x768**, which is the minimum resolution of Windows 8. These are also one of the best ways to promote your game, so ensure you take some great screenshots that show off the fun and appeal of your game.

There are a few ways to take a screenshot of your game. If you're testing in the simulator you can use the screenshot icon on the right toolbar of the simulator to take the screenshot. If not, you can use Windows Key + Prt Scr SysRq to take a screenshot of your entire screen, and then use that (or edit it if you have multiple monitors). Screenshots taken with either of these tools can be found in the Screenshots folder within your Pictures library.

There are two other small pieces of information that are required during this stage: **Copyright Info** and **Support contact info**. For the support info, an e-mail address will usually suffice.

At this point you can also include your website and, if applicable to your game, a link to the privacy policy included in your game. Note that if you require a privacy policy, it must be included in two places: your game, and the privacy policy field on this form.

The last items you may want to add here are promotional images. These images are intended for use in store promotions and allow Microsoft to easily feature your game with larger promotional imagery in prominent locations within the store. If you are serious about maximizing the reach of your game, you will want to include these images. If you don't, the number of places your game can be featured will be reduced. At a minimum the **414x180 px** image should be included if you want some form of promotion.

Now you're almost done! The next section allows you to leave notes for the testing team. This is where you would leave test account details for any features in your game that require an account so that they can test those features. This is also the location to leave any notes about testing in case there are situations where you can point out any features that might not be obvious. In certain situations you may have an exemption from Microsoft for a certification requirement; this would be where you include that exemption.

When every step has been completed and you have tick marks in all of the stages, the **Submit for Certification** button will unlock, allowing you to complete your submission and send it off for certification. At this stage a number of automated tests will run before human testers will try your game on a variety of devices to ensure it fits the requirements for the store.

If all goes well, you will receive an email notifying you of your successful certification and, depending on if you set the release date as ASAP, you will find your game in the store a few hours later (it may take a few hours to appear in the store once you receive an email informing you that your game or app is in the store).

Certification tips

Your first stop should be the certification requirements page, which lists all of the current requirements your game will be tested for: http://msdn.microsoft.com/ en-us/library/windows/apps/hh694083.aspx.

There are some requirements that you should take note of, and in this section we'll take a look at ways to help ensure you pass those requirements.

Privacy

The first of course is the privacy policy. As mentioned before, if your game collects any sort of personal information, you will need that policy in two places:

- In full text within the game
- Accessible through an Internet link

The default app template generated by Visual Studio automatically enables the Internet capability, and by simply having that enabled you require a privacy policy. If you aren't connecting to the Internet at all in your game, you should always ensure that none of the Internet options are enabled before you package your game.

If you share any personal information, then you need to provide players with a method of opting in to the sharing. This could be done by gating the functionality behind a login screen. Note that this functionality can be locked away, and the requirement doesn't demand that you find a way to remain fully functional even if the user opts out.

Features

One requirement is that your game support both touch input and keyboard/mouse input. You can easily support this by using an input system like the one described in this book; however, by supporting touch input you get mouse input for free and technically fulfill this requirement. It's all about how much effort you want to put into the experience your player will have, and that's why including gamepad input is recommended as some players may want to use a connected Xbox 360 gamepad for their input device in games.

Legacy APIs

Although your game might run while using legacy APIs, it won't pass certification. This is checked through an automated test that also occurs during the WACK testing process, so you can easily check if you have used any illegal APIs. This often arises in third party libraries that make use of parts of the standard IO library such as the console, or the insecure versions of functions such as `strcpy` or `fopen`. Some of these APIs don't exist in WinRT for good reason; the console, for example, just doesn't exist, so calling APIs that work directly with the console makes no sense, and isn't allowed.

Debug

Another issue that may arise through the use of third-party libraries is that some of them may be compiled in debug mode. This could present issues at runtime for your app, and the packaging system will happily include these when compiling your game, unless it has to compile them itself. This is detected by the WACK and can be resolved by finding a release mode version, or recompiling the library.

WACK

The final tip is: run WACK. This kit quickly and easily finds most of the issues you may encounter during certification, and you see the issues immediately rather than waiting for the game to fail during the certification process. Your final step before submitting to the store should be to run WACK, and even while developing it's a good idea to compile in release mode and run the tests to just make sure nothing is broken.

Summary

By now you should know how to submit your game to the store, and get through certification with few to no issues. We've looked at what you require for the store including imagery and metadata, as well as how to make use of the Windows Application Certification Kit to find problems early on and fix them up without waiting hours or days for certification to fail your game.

One area unique to games that we have covered in this chapter is game ratings. If you're developing your game for certain markets where ratings are required, or if you are developing children's games, you may need to get a rating certificate, and hopefully you have an idea of where to look to do this.

Next steps

The one topic we avoided in this chapter involved making money from your game, which is a whole chapter in itself. In our final chapter we will take a look at the options you have to sell your game, as well as the options available to provide in-app purchases like those seen in many modern freemium games. The Windows Store also offers a unique trial system that allows you to easily add a trial mode to your game to help players decide if they want to pay by getting to experience a taste of your game for free. If you're looking to make some money from your game, you'll want to read through the next chapter before you submit your game to the store.

9
Monetization

Through all of the previous chapters we have looked at how to create a game and get it into the store. In many cases developers will stop there and put the game out for free. One of the major benefits of the app and mobile gaming boom comes from the monetary benefit you can gain. Even traditional-selling models have been shaken up and adapted to take advantage of the technology people used to consume.

Through this chapter we will take a look at the options available to you so you can hopefully make some money from your work, as well as some options available to encourage others to buy your game. We'll focus on the following topics in particular:

- Selling your game
- Trial versions
- Monetization models
- In-app purchases

Once you're done with this chapter you will be equipped to dive into game development on Windows 8 and start creating and selling your own games.

Selling your games

Like any app store, the Windows Store allows you to sell your app or game, and handles the transaction for you, allowing you to focus on developing the game and raking in the profits. To handle this, they take a share of each sale before tax, and then collect the rest and pay the developer in lump sum payments, usually based on a time period or accumulated threshold. To set a price for your game, we need to return to the **Windows Store Dashboard** and edit our game release. Inside there you will find the **Selling Details** section, which is where we can define details like the price, the trial, and the markets that the game will be sold in.

As mentioned in the previous chapter, the markets that you sell your game in will be affected by the ratings you have. Some markets require a rating for a game to be sold, so be sure to take a look at the provided information in the **Ratings** section of the dashboard to see if your game complies or which markets you need to remove from the **Selling Details** page.

For the price of your game, you have a large selection of options to choose from. If you want to put your game out there for free you can, or if you want to charge $999 you can (although that might not be the best idea if you want to sell a copy). The price can sometimes be a difficult decision to make, and getting it wrong can impact sales; however, sticking close to the industry standard will usually keep you safe.

As this is a mobile platform, you need to consider that the pricing structure for mobile games is very different from the traditional retail pricing. A race to the bottom has led to many consumers expecting the 99c price point for games, and anything higher than that requires a bit of content to justify the extra cost. Thankfully, this has shifted away as larger companies push into the market with higher price points; however, you should not expect consumers to be happy with prices over $10-$15, unless your game has a lot of amazing content. To get around this limitation, mobile games have started to rely on in-app purchases to make up the extra revenue; we'll take a look at how you can add that later in this chapter.

Once you have decided on your price, you need to set it using the provided drop-down menu. If you are charging for your game, you also have the option of setting a trial period. There are two ways you can provide a trial game to your customers. The first is to use the Windows Store API to check if your game is running in trial mode, and then alter your content accordingly. This takes a little more effort; however, you can tailor the experience to try and encourage a purchase (also known as a conversion). We'll take a look at this in the next section.

The other technique is much easier, and lets you just specify a trial period in which the player can enjoy your game as if they had bought it. However, at the end of the trial period the game will be locked out automatically and the player will be prompted to purchase the game. This is managed by the store and is done automatically for you based on the period you specify, which means you can easily add in a short trial of the game for potential customers to experience, without actually touching your
game code.

The downside here is that, if your game can be experienced completely within the trial period, they may not feel the need to buy the game. You can, however, combine both techniques and allow the store to manage the trial time-out, while you restrict features based on the trial mode flag in the store API. No matter which path you go down, consider the experience of the players and make it something that encourages them to buy the full game.

The final thing that you need to do here is select the markets you want to sell in. Just check the boxes next to each market you want. The price that your game will be listed for in each market is calculated based on the price you set earlier. This is relevant for any advertising or marketing you want to do, where you can localize the price and currency for the market you're advertising to. Ultimately it won't make a difference, as the store handles conversion and provides the profits from the base price, so you don't have to worry about conversion rates.

Monetization models

You'll notice that I mentioned in-app purchases earlier, and different ways of selling or making money from games. The race to the bottom has led to many developers taking a different approach to profiting from their games. We'll take a look at three models that you can use to make some money from your games.

The freemium model

The **freemium** model provides the game to the player for free, and instead makes money by selling functionality or content inside the game itself. This has become a popular model because it allows players to try the game and sell the game in parts, or even sell the game for a combined value that is much higher than the game is worth. To accomplish this in Windows 8, you would have to set the price of your game to Free, and then use in-app purchases to unlock content for the player to use.

This model is great if you have a lot of modular content within a single game experience that can be sold separately, such as levels or episodes. You may also elect to create an in-game currency that the player can use to buy this content or other bonuses. Often, this will be done with coins that the player can buy in predefined bundles. Some games will have two in-game currencies, one that can be acquired in the game, and one that can only be bought. By offering content in both of these currencies, you allow players to get that content by playing the game a lot, which works for people with plenty of time.

For those with less time, you can offer a cheaper deal that lets them get the content with the special premium currency; however, they ultimately need to pay for it. Some games will allow for conversion from the premium currency for use in the game. For example, a city-building game might allow the player to buy extra resources to build more, or they might allow the player to pay to accelerate the construction of buildings and save time.

The traditional model

This model is what you're used to in most retail games, and the simplest. You set a price up front, and the consumer pays that price to get the entire game. You can easily do this using the techniques mentioned earlier, and if you ever want to expand the game, you still have the option of providing paid content packs (commonly known as **Downloadable Content** or **DLC**), or release a paid sequel.

As the experience should always be your first priority, you should remember that, as the players are paying upfront, they won't want to see extra content being sold at launch as this is often seen as an attempt to just leech some more money from them. In this case you want to ensure that any DLC you release is provided at a point after launch, even if you include the framework and menus to buy it in your released game.

The hybrid model

Another option is to combine the two, and provide the content for your game for an upfront fee, while providing optional boosts to the player at an extra cost. By doing this you let the players who have time and want to sit and play the game do so without paying any more, and those who want to speed things up pay a little bit for the privilege, which many will prefer and appreciate.

In all of the given cases you need to consider the impact of any boosts or bonuses on gameplay, especially in multiplayer games. By allowing players to purchase items that impact gameplay, you can potentially upset the balance in a game, which many might feel is unfair if they are unable to afford the extra cost.

Another issue you need to consider surrounds young players. While in-app purchases are allowed and are okay for games oriented towards young players, you will need to consider that many won't use it. Windows requires password verification before a purchase is made; however, if you're using your own system for purchases, you will need to be careful.

The trial mode

So you want to sell your game upfront, but also want to give players a taste of the game so that they can be encouraged to buy your game instead of ignoring it. This can be accomplished using the **Trial mode flag** provided by the **Windows Store API** in WinRT.

Even if you want to offer your full game as a time-limited trial using the built-in functionality in the store, you might still want to add in some screens or messages to encourage the player to buy the game. For that, you need to know if the game is a trial, or if the player has purchased it.

This can be easily accessed using the following lines:

```
auto trial = Windows::ApplicationModel::Store::CurrentApp-
>LicenseInformation->IsTrial;
auto trialActive = Windows::ApplicationModel::Store::CurrentApp-
>LicenseInformation->IsActive;
if (trial && trialActive)
  // We are in trial mode and it hasn't expired
```

You'll notice here that we retrieve the IsTrial flag as well as the IsActive flag. The IsTrial flag just indicates if the license is for a trial game or a full game. It does not, however, indicate if the license has expired or been revoked. This can be checked using the IsActive flag, which lets us know if the license (full or trial) is active and valid. When used in combination we can determine if the trial is running fine and is in fact a trial.

The other thing we should do at this stage is also subscribe to the LicenseChanged event, which notifies us if the player has changed the license by purchasing the game, or if the trial has expired while the player was playing. By responding to this we can alter the game appropriately without requiring the player to forcefully terminate the game and relaunch it. This enables us to get the player to switch to the store while he or she is playing, buy the game, and then switch back into the game, which will have recognized their purchase and unlocked any full game features.

One of the things you want to do if you're in a trial mode is display some kind of message screen to the users asking them to buy, or at least offer them an easy buy button that lets them purchase your game without returning to the store. To do this you should also show the current price of your game before they buy.

Traditionally you might hardcode this, and then have to issue a game update every time you want to change the price, but using the store API you can retrieve details about the store listing, and use that information to construct your up-sell page. This is shown in the code snippet that follows:

```
concurrency::task<ListingInformation^> listingTask(CurrentApp::
  LoadListingInformationAsync());
listingTask.wait();
try
{
  auto listing = listingTask.get();
  Platform::String^ price = listing->FormattedPrice;
}
catch (Platform::Exception^ e)
{
  // Operation failed, unable to connect maybe?
}
```

To retrieve the price of the game, we need to get the listing information, which contains details such as the name, price, rating, and description, as shown in the store.

As we are retrieving this information from the store, we need to be able to connect to the Internet, which means that this is an asynchronous operation, and it can fail. These failures will be surfaced as exceptions that will appear to your game when you call the `get()` method on the task. In the earlier example we aren't using the continuation system; instead, we are waiting for the task to complete.

The provided price is formatted for you in the local currency, so that you can use it immediately in your user interface.

Once the player is ready to buy, you just need to call the `RequestAppPurchaseAsync()` method to carry out the purchase and Windows will take care of the rest. This is shown in the code snippet that follows:

```
concurrency::task<Platform::String^> purchaseTask(CurrentApp::
  RequestAppPurchaseAsync(false));
purchaseTask.wait();
try
{
  auto receipt = purchaseTask.get();
}
catch (Platform::Exception^ e)
{
  // An error occurred
}
```

If desired, you can also request a receipt, which you can use with your own systems as required using the Boolean parameter on the `RequestAppPurchaseAsync()` method. Whether you request a receipt or not, you should still call the `get()` method on the task so that any errors can be raised as exceptions and you can report success appropriately. If you pass `false` to `RequestAppPurchaseAsync()`, you will not receive a receipt, but the `get()` method won't crash either.

Later in this chapter, we'll take a look at how to use a simulator to test this code out before you submit to the store.

In-app purchases

The popular option for mobile games these days is the **in-app purchase**. This is a product that can be bought inside the game that can exist perpetually or be consumed and repurchased, unlocking or providing whatever you want.

You will begin by creating products in the store dashboard. Here you have to define the price and expiry time for the product. When the player buys the product, it is active for the amount of time you specify, which could be forever if you choose that option. Take note of the IDs at this point as we will use those later.

A consumable is a product that the users can buy as many times as they want. It gets the name from the fact that the product is consumed immediately, as opposed to a durable, which lasts perpetually (or until expired). Consumables are often used for coin purchases where the player might want to buy some coins and then immediately buy some more. Windows 8 does not support this scenario as the minimum expiry time for a product is 24 hours. This is not a problem as we can work around this limitation, which we will look at after we understand how to retrieve and purchase the in-app products.

As you specify the product ID, you can feel free to skip retrieving the product list from the store and instead insert it directly into your game. This is often the best route as it lets you perfect the display and icons for each product; however, in some cases (as outlined in our workaround) we may want to separate the display of the products from the products that are actually available.

One other thing to note is that the users need to be running the full version of the game before they can use in-app purchases. If you are selling your game then you need to ensure that they have active, non-trial licenses, and if not you need to prompt them to purchase the game. Once they have the game, you can request product purchases and proceed as normal.

To retrieve the list of products, we need to retrieve them from the product listing acquired using the `LoadListingInformationAsync()` method, which is shown as follows:

```
concurrency::task<ListingInformation^> listingTask(CurrentApp::LoadLis
tingInformationAsync());
listingTask.wait();
try
{
  auto listing = listingTask.get();
  auto products = listing->ProductListings;
  auto productDetails = products->Lookup("PRODUCT_ID");
}
catch (Platform::Exception^ e)
{
  // Operation failed, unable to connect maybe?
}
```

The `ListingInformation` will provide you with a list of `ProductListing` objects (mapped to strings) that provide you with the ID of the product and the price, formatted to the locale of the user.

Once the players have chosen what they want to buy, and they have licenses for the full game, you will want to check if they already have licenses for the product. If they do, the purchase will fail. To check this, you can retrieve the product licenses from the `LicenseInformation` object that you learned how to retrieve earlier. This is shown in the code snippet that follows:

```
auto license = CurrentApp::LicenseInformation;
auto productLicense = license->ProductLicenses-
>Lookup("PRODUCT_ID");
```

Just like the application license, this `ProductLicense` contains an `IsActive` property as well as an expiration date so that you can determine if they have valid and active licenses for the product.

Once you know a player has a license and is fine to buy it, you can request the purchase, which will inform Windows that it should display the details and the required screens to let the user purchase the product.

```
concurrency::task<Platform::String^> buyTask(CurrentApp::
  RequestProductPurchaseAsync("PRODUCT_ID", false));
buyTask.wait();
try
{
  auto result = buyTask.get();
  auto success = CurrentApp::LicenseInformation->ProductLicenses-
>Lookup("PRODUCT_ID")->IsActive;
}
catch (Platform::Exception^ e)
{
  // Purchase failed
}
```

In the `RequestProductPurchaseAsync()` command you need to provide the string ID for the product as specified in the store dashboard, as well as a Boolean representing whether you want to receive a receipt from the purchase for your own tracking. Once it is done you can check the `IsActive` flag on the corresponding license and verify that everything has been processed appropriately.

Once that is done successfully you can grant the user access to whatever your in-app purchase provides, and continue as normal.

 Remember that you don't have to use the Windows Store to implement in-app purchases. If you prefer to use an alternate payment provider you are allowed to do this, and Microsoft does not require a cut of the profits in this case.

The consumables

Consumables aren't officially supported by the Windows Store for Windows 8. The solution to this lack of functionality is rather simple. We will start by creating a number of products in the dashboard with the same identifier, except each one must have an increasing number appended to it; for example:

- IAP-1
- IAP-2
- IAP-3

Once those are in place, we need to use a combination of the given techniques to go through each one until we find one that hasn't been bought, and buy that. Each product should have a minimum expiry of 1 day, so that effectively they can buy N copies of the same product in a single day.

First retrieve the listing information so we know what products are in the store:

```
concurrency::task<ListingInformation^> getlisting(CurrentApp::LoadList
  ingInformationAsync());
getlisting.wait();
try
{
  auto listing = getlisting.get();
int count = 1;
auto transformedId = identifier + L"-" + count;
while (listing->ProductListings->Lookup(transformedId))
```

Now construct your identifier (of type `Platform::String^`) to match what you have placed in the dashboard, including the index, which in this case is represented by an `int` that we have named `count`. After that we will use a loop, inside which we will add our purchase code. Each iteration will perform a lookup of the product. If it exists with the current identifier, then we can try and buy it; if not then we have run out of products for that identifier, and if by now we haven't purchased the product, then we need to fail out and maybe indicate that the player should return the next day. This is shown in the following code snippet:

```
if (!license->ProductLicenses->Lookup(transformedId)->IsActive)
{
  // Product hasn't been purchased yet
  concurrency::task<Platform::String^>
purchaseTask(CurrentApp::RequestProductPurchaseAsync(transformedId,
false));
  purchaseTask.wait();
  if (license->ProductLicenses->Lookup(transformedId)->IsActive)
    // return indicating success
}
count++;
transformedId = TransformConsumable(identifier, count);
```

This block of code handles most of the work. Here we check if the product has been purchased, and if it hasn't then we can request a purchase. Assuming that succeeds, then we are done and we don't need to keep looping. If the product has already been purchased then we increase the index and try again with the new identifier.

Testing with the simulator

Much of what we have looked at uses the `CurrentApp` class, which connects to the associated Windows Store account to process the transactions. This requires that any IAP products exist in the dashboard, and really gets in the way of any sort of testing before you submit your game. To get around this, the `CurrentAppSimulator` class allows us to test the different scenarios to ensure that our trial mode and the IAP code work fine. The simulator also allows you to test without even creating the app in the store dashboard, instead using a local XML file that describes the game and any IAP products that can be sold to populate the different listings and license details.

To get started with this, we need to replace all instances of the `CurrentApp` class with the `CurrentAppSimulator`. This can be easily accomplished using a preprocessor directive for `DEBUG` builds, and some `typedefs` to abstract the `CurrentApp` and `CurrentAppSimulator` based on the build configuration.

```
#if DEBUG
typedef Windows::ApplicationModel::Store::CurrentAppSimulator
StoreApp;
#else
typedef Windows::ApplicationModel::Store::CurrentApp StoreApp;
#endif
```

In this case we rename the object to `StoreApp`, and let the preprocessor handle choosing the correct class to use.

Now we need to load in the XML file that describes our simulation product(s). Where you choose to include this XML file is up to you however, the simplest place is to include it in the build until you're ready to submit your game, and then remove it before doing so.

To load the file, we need to manually load the `StorageFile` that represents it. If you're looking to retrieve from the app package, you can do so using the `Windows::ApplicationModel::Package::Current->InstalledLocation`, which will give you a `StorageFolder` representing the root of your installation directory. Once you have that, just retrieve your XML file and use it in the following block of code:

```
concurrency::task<void> reloadTask(CurrentAppSimulator::
  ReloadSimulatorAsync(xmlFile));
reloadTask.wait();
```

Now that the file has been loaded in, you can interact with the simulator as if it were a `CurrentApp`; however, when a purchase is requested, a debug dialog will appear, allowing you to select which response the store should provide. This would be where you test how your app works if a purchase fails or succeeds.

The XML file has a simple format, with a `CurrentApp` node for the root, and then two child nodes, as follows:

- The `ListingInformation` node
- The `LicenseInformation` node

You can find a sample simulator file and full reference at

`http://msdn.microsoft.com/en-us/library/windows/apps/windows.applicationmodel.store.currentappsimulator.aspx`.

Let's take a look at the `ListingInformation` node, which defines the same data that you would specify in the store dashboard:

```xml
<?xml version="1.0" encoding="utf-16" ?>
<CurrentApp>
  <ListingInformation />
  <LicenseInformation />
</CurrentApp>
```

There are two different items that can appear inside the `ListingInformation` section: the `App`, and one or more `Product` nodes. As you would expect, the `App` node describes the details about the app, such as the App ID, Store Link, Age Rating, and Price for the simulator market (which is also defined here). The `Product` node describes a single in-app purchase with similar (but less) information compared to the `App` node, as follows:

```xml
<App>
  <AppId>6492e999-74b3-4a30-92a7-76502f4700bf</AppId>
  <LinkUri>Link to the store here</LinkUri>
  <CurrentMarket>en-us</CurrentMarket>
  <AgeRating>12</AgeRating>
  <MarketData xml:lang="en-us">
    <Name>Sample Game</Name>
    <Description>Sample Description</Description>
    <Price>1.49</Price>
    <CurrencySymbol>$</CurrencySymbol>
    <CurrencyCode>USD</CurrencyCode>
  </MarketData>
</App>
```

As shown earlier, we specify which market the simulator is pretending to be in. With this we can test rendering for other locales as required. Along with this we provide the store information required to fill out the `ListingInformation` for the app, including the price.

The other set of nodes that can sit inside `ListingInformation` are the `Product` nodes, defined as shown:

```
<Product ProductId="product1">
  <MarketData xml:lang="en-us">
    <Name>Product 1</Name>
    <Price>1.99</Price>
    <CurrencySymbol>$</CurrencySymbol>
    <CurrencyCode>USD</CurrencyCode>
  </MarketData>
</Product>
```

You can have multiples of these nodes, one for each IAP product that you want to provide to your players. Similar to our app we will provide information about the price and market currency, although we don't need to provide much more than that, just the `ProductId` inside the `Product` tag, which represents the ID we provide when requesting a purchase or looking up the details.

The final section is the `LicenseInformation`, which allows us to set up some preconditions that help test our game in situations where the player is running a trial (or an expired trial) versus the full version, or a situation where the player already has IAP products purchased and valid on startup.

Just like the `ListingInformation` elements, there are `App` and `Product` nodes in this; however, the amount of information required is heavily reduced. For the app description we just need to indicate if this is a trial, and if the license is active, as described earlier. This is shown in the following piece of code:

```
<App>
  <IsActive>true</IsActive>
  <IsTrial>false</IsTrial>
</App>
```

The `Product` node is just as simple:

```
<Product ProductId="product1">
  <IsActive>true</IsActive>
<ExpirationDate>2014-01-01T00:00:00.00Z</ExpirationDate>
</Product>
```

As you can see you just need to provide an ID to associate with the listing, and then the values for `IsActive` and the `ExpirationDate`. The expiration value is optional, so if you have a product that doesn't expire you don't need to include a value.

Summary

Over the course of this book you have learned the techniques required to get started developing native Direct3D games for Windows 8. We've looked at the different components of a game and how to use the Windows 8 APIs to enhance your game past the standard gameplay. You should also understand how to get your game through certification and into the store.

In this chapter we looked at how to sell your game in the store, and the different APIs available to manage the trial versions as well as in-app purchases. You should hopefully also have a better understanding of the monetization models common in modern game development and, using the techniques provided, be able to apply them to make some money from your game.

If you're looking to take your knowledge further and jump into another dimension, be sure to read *Appendix, Adding the Third Dimension*, which covers basic 3D rendering, the next step in your game development journey.

The important thing is to get out there, make, and publish your games. Be sure to take advantage of the features native to Windows 8 to create a unique and rich experience for players. Direct3D provides a lot of power, and it has never been easier to use now that we can work with technologies such as C++11 and C++/CX to develop games.

My final tip would be to engage with your local Microsoft Developer team. Microsoft has a number of Developer Platform Evangelism teams around the world with the sole focus of working with you to help you do cool things on Microsoft platforms. If you want to try and get your game featured in local or worldwide markets as well as get any assistance, go straight to the source and get in contact. You never know what opportunities they may unlock, and at the very least they'll be more than happy to provide some free advertising for great games on the Windows platform.

Go forth, use what you've learned to make some awesome games for Windows, and hopefully make some money while you're at it!

Adding the Third Dimension

In the previous chapters you have been working on a 2D game, and DirectXTK hides away a lot of the complexity of making a 2D game in a 3D world. Most big-budget modern games make use of 3D instead of 2D for most of the action, to create immersive experiences that in many cases try to look as realistic as possible.

3D itself is not much more complicated than working in 2D; however, because we're working with Direct3D directly now, there is some extra complexity and concepts that you need to learn to understand how everything fits together.

In this appendix we're going to take a crash course in 3D rendering by looking at the different concepts involved, from vertices to shaders, and how they all fit together to put a 3D object on the screen.

We will cover the following topics:

- Vertices and triangles
- Indices
- 3D cameras
- DirectXMath
- Buffers
- Shaders (vertex and pixel)
- Input layouts
- Drawing the model

If you've skipped back to this section and aren't familiar with the Direct3D pipeline and how to set it up, be sure to go back and read *Chapter 1, Getting Started with Direct3D*, before you continue.

Vertices and triangles

All 3D models consist of a collection of points in space called **vertices**. These vertices (singular: vertex) define the shape of the model when combined. Each vertex is a coordinate in space, represented in vector form. They can, however, also contain further information, such as the following:

- Color
- Normal
- Texture coordinates
- Anything else you need to draw the model

These vertices are used by the GPU to draw the model; however, the GPU by itself has no way of understanding how they relate to each other, and how to draw the correct model. This is resolved by arranging vertices into the most basic shape possible: a triangle. If you consider that one vertex alone as a point, which along with a second forms a line, then a third vertex creates a triangle, which is the simplest polygon you can create. The GPU can then draw these triangles by taking the vertices, three at a time, and using those values to generate an area to draw.

A model created in a 3D editing program can have thousands of these vertices, all forming triangles that define the final shape. The following diagram shows one such instance:

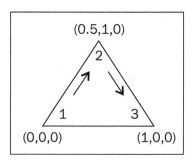

The more vertices drawn, the more work the GPU has to do, and the larger impact on performance a model takes. There is also no point drawing vertices that are completely hidden by other triangles on the same model.

This is where **backface culling** comes into play. Backface culling allows the GPU to only draw triangles facing the camera, saving time on triangles that are on the other side of the object and usually invisible. Now how would you determine if a triangle is on the back of an object, when the object could have any orientation, and the camera could be in any position?

This is done by ensuring that all triangles facing the camera have their vertices specified in a clockwise-winding order, which is demonstrated in the diagram that follows. When sent to the GPU, the order is evaluated and if the vertices are submitted in a counter-clockwise fashion, they are discarded as they should be facing away from the camera, and are most likely hidden.

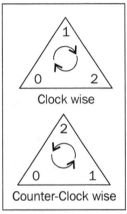

Winding order

This can be disabled or changed using the custom states that are set on the GPU. By disabling or reversing the winding order that gets culled, you can tailor the behavior of the backface culling system to allow for different rendering techniques.

Indices

You may have noticed that we need to render each triangle with a new set of vertices, which can lead to a lot of vertices sitting in exactly the same place. This is fairly inefficient at high triangle counts, and takes up a lot of memory, especially when you have multiple blocks of information stored within a vertex. We can get around this using a concept similar to array indexing. We will start by providing an array of vertices to the GPU; however, instead of defining the order to draw the triangles in the same array, we just provide single vertex entries for each point.

The GPU then uses this alongside an array of indices to define the layout of the triangles. We will save a lot of memory by defining each point by a single integer rather than a full vertex for each triangle corner.

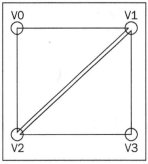

Indices for a quad

If we want to draw the given quad without an index buffer, we will need the following:

```
Vec3(0, 0, 0)
Vec3(1, 0, 0)
Vec3(0, 1, 0)
Vec3(0, 1, 0)
Vec3(1, 0, 0)
Vec3(1, 1, 0)
```

Now if we use an index buffer, we can just define four vertices and let the index buffer define the triangles, as follows:

```
Vec3(0, 0, 0)
Vec3(1, 0, 0)
Vec3(0, 1, 0)
Vec3(1, 1, 0)

Indices = [0, 1, 2, 2, 1, 3]
```

If you want to create a cube, you just need to define the eight points of the cube and use indices in the right order to create the triangles. In large models with thousands or tens of thousands of vertices this can save quite a lot of memory, and allows dynamic changes to the model without affecting the original vertex list.

[Remember that you can never have a negative index in an array, so Direct3D only supports unsigned integer values.]

Cameras

We have all of this data in our 3D world, representing objects and other visuals that we need to get onto the screen; however, how do we go about describing what is in our limited view? For this, we need a camera. A camera in this case is a virtual representation of our view into the world. It stores information about where we are, what direction we are looking in, and how we need to transform the third dimension so that it either looks real or useful. Using cameras, we can also define part of the gameplay. Players will play a first person shooter (where the camera is in the head of the player character) differently than a third person shooter, where the camera sits over the shoulder of the player character. Back in *Chapter 2, Drawing 2D Sprites*, I described the two different projections we use to do that transformation: the **perspective** and **orthographic** projections.

By combining all of the data into a single matrix, we have a nice and easy way to transform all of the different vertices through the different spaces until we reach the correct location on the 2D screen to display the pixels.

Now we will take a quick look at the different spaces, and how we can use a camera to go from a collection of vertices to pixels on the screen.

The vertices begin in **Model Space**. This is a coordinate space where all of the vertices are relative to an origin that was specified when the model was created. For example, the origin of a character model could be at the center of its body; however, that character may be nowhere near [0,0,0] when placed in the world. We can use this space to work with the single model without worrying about the fact that we may use this model at a distant location in the world.

These vertices are then transformed into World Space by using matrices derived from the position, rotation, and scale of the model. Now we are putting this object in context with everything else in the world.

Once it has its place within the world, we need to think about how to get everything relative to the camera. The next step is to transform the vertices into View Space, which is a coordinate space relative to the camera (the camera is at [0,0,0]).

Now that we have everything relative to the camera, we need to project the vertices in front of us onto the 2D screen plane, which transforms the vertices into Screen Space (also known as Post Projection Space). Now we have vertices in their correct locations relative to the screen (with an origin in the center of the screen), allowing the API to handle the final transforms and clipping required to get a 2D pixel grid for rendering.

By combining each of these transformations together we form a **World-View-Projection transform** that takes a vertex right through to screen space. This is done within the vertex shader, which will be explained later on.

Direct3D doesn't have any functions to do that for you, but **DirectXMath** (also provided in the Windows 8 SDK) has plenty of functions to do the math and ensure you get the right result.

DirectXMath

Although this topic is too big for the scope of this appendix, we'll work through the basics so that you understand how to get started.

For more information on DirectXMath, visit:
`http://msdn.microsoft.com/en-us/library/windows/desktop/ee415574.`

All the points (and vertices) are represented by using an array of three floats called a Vector, which represents the x, y, and z axes. In DirectXMath this is represented by the `DirectX::XMFLOAT3` structure.

For simplicity I'll avoid using the DirectX namespace in front of all the references, but, don't forget that all of DirectXMath sits within that namespace—so be sure to ensure you reference it in some way.

Most operations on this data are done by first converting the `XMFLOAT3` to an `XMVECTOR`, which represents the **SIMD (Single Instruction, Multiple Data)** units on the CPU. Two simple functions provide you with a way to get information in and out of `XMVECTOR`, shown as follows:

```
XMFLOAT3 start = XMFLOAT3(1, 1, 1);
XMVECTOR vec = XMLoadFloat3(&start);

XMFLOAT3 end;
XMStoreFloat3(&end, vec);
```

As shown, we **Load** the `XMFLOAT3` into the `XMVECTOR`, and **Store** the result of our operations back into the `XMFLOAT3`.

But what about the matrices that we need for the camera? Those are provided using the XMMATRIX data type. In most cases you will use a couple of key methods to create and manipulate these matrices, as shown in the following code snippet:

```
XMMATRIX XMMatrixMultiply(XMMATRIX M1, XMMATRIX M2);
// World & View Matrices
XMMATRIX XMMatrixTranslation(float x, float y, float z);
XMMATRIX XMMatrixScaling(float x, float y, float z);
XMMATRIX XMMatrixRotationRollPitchYaw(float pitch, float yaw,
    float roll);
XMMATRIX XMMatrixPerspectiveFovRH(float fov, float aspectRatio,
    float nearZ, float farZ);
```

Most of these are straightforward, but, the last one may have some new concepts.

A **perspective projection** requires some information to correctly warp the scene so that we have vanishing points and a horizon. To do this, we need to provide the **field of view** (fov) and aspectRatio of the camera. In this particular case the field of view refers to the vertical field of view rather than the horizontal field of view that you may be used to.

The nearZ and farZ parameters refer to how far the two clipping planes are from the position of the camera. A **clipping plane** is the point where objects are no longer rendered. This prevents weird-rendering artefacts when models cross over the position of the camera, and allows you to define the farthest point from the camera — which is required for the depth parameter that is stored as a value from 0.0f to 1.0f.

These parameters combine to give you a matrix that defines a shape called a **frustum**, which contains everything visible in the scene.

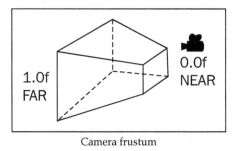

Camera frustum

Buffers

Now we need to take these vertices and indices and get them into arrays that the GPU can understand. This is done through the use of buffers, which refer to blocks of memory that the GPU can use for a variety of different tasks.

Direct3D provides a couple of different types of buffers, each with their own purpose in the pipeline. The most commonly used buffers include the following:

- Vertex buffers
- Index buffers
- Constant buffers

As you may have gathered, we use vertex and index buffers to store the data we need for rendering.

Building the vertex and index buffers

To create these buffers, we need to build up an array of the data, being careful to control the layout of each vertex. Later on we'll tell the GPU how to read the data, so we can make sure that we know how it will be laid out in memory. To do this, we need to create a structure definition that outlines the layout of each vertex. A simple vertex structure could look like the following:

```
typedef struct PositionNormalVertex
{
  XMFLOAT3 Position;
  XMFLOAT3 Normal;
} PositionNormalVertex;
```

This structure defines a position and a normal for each vertex. At a minimum each vertex requires a position; however, most lighting techniques also require a normal for the lighting equation. If the model has been created in a 3D editing package, you may need to check what vertex parameters your importer gives you, and ensure that you remove the parameters you won't be using (alternatively, you can provide a vertex structure that matches what you have imported).

An index buffer is simply an array of integers, so we don't need to do anything special before creating it.

Now that we have the data we need to import, we need to create the buffers. For this we need to create a D3D11_BUFFER_DESC structure to describe the buffer for the API. Following is the layout of the D3D11_BUFFER_DESC structure, as outlined by MSDN:

```
typedef struct D3D11_BUFFER_DESC {
  UINT        ByteWidth;
  D3D11_USAGE Usage;
  UINT        BindFlags;
  UINT        CPUAccessFlags;
  UINT        MiscFlags;
  UINT        StructureByteStride;
} D3D11_BUFFER_DESC;
```

(`http://msdn.microsoft.com/en-us/library/windows/desktop/ff476092.`)

To start with, `ByteWidth` describes the total size of the buffer in bytes, which would be `sizeof(PositionNormalVertex) * NumberOfVertices`.

Usage specifies how we intend to use the buffer. We choose this value based on how frequently we intend to use the buffer. The possible options are as follows:

- `D3D11_USAGE_IMMUTABLE`: Most of the time you should use the `D3D11_USAGE_IMMUTABLE` for your vertex buffers. This tells the GPU that you won't be changing the buffer, and it can optimize for higher performance using that information. This option makes the buffer read-only for the GPU only; the CPU cannot access this buffer after creation.

- `D3D11_USAGE_DYNAMIC`: This lets the GPU know that you intend to change the buffer, potentially each frame, and so safeguards need to be put in place to ensure that you can safely access and update the data, while trying to maintain performance. This option is read-only for the GPU, and write-only for the CPU.

 Only the `Map()` method may access a buffer created with this setting.

- `D3D11_USAGE_DEFAULT`: This describes a buffer that gives read and write access to the GPU. This is the most common choice for a lot of buffers, however, in the case of vertex and index buffers this is not the most optimal choice.

- `D3D11_USAGE_STAGING`: Finally `D3D11_USAGE_STAGING` describes a buffer that will be used for the staging update method. This is when you use an intermediate buffer to update a buffer on the GPU through a resource copy. This method has a performance benefit and avoids costly synchronization blocks, at the cost of extra memory.

As a vertex buffer rarely changes after creation, it is strongly recommended that you use the `D3D11_USAGE_IMMUTABLE` for those buffers, and pass in the data during the creation call.

Moving on, `BindFlags` describes what the buffer will be, and consequently where it will be bound in the pipeline. A handy enumeration makes it easy to set this value and, while there are a few options to choose from, we only really care about the `D3D11_BIND_VERTEX_BUFFER` and `D3D11_BIND_INDEX_BUFFER`.

CPUAccessFlags tells the API how the CPU will access the buffer after creation, allowing for optimizations based on what you require. In most cases you won't need CPU access so you can just set this to zero; however, if you want access you will need to apply a logical OR operation to set the flag as desired. The D3D11_CPU_ACCESS_ FLAG enumeration provides you with two options for this setting: D3D11_CPU_ ACCESS_WRITE and D3D11_CPU_ACCESS_READ.

MiscFlags allows you to set some extra flags using a logical OR operation on values from the D3D11_RESOURCE_MISC_FLAG enumeration. In most cases you will just set this to zero.

Finally StructureByteStride tells the API how large each element in your array is. This is simply a sizeof(VertexPositionNormal); in our case, however, set this as required in your situation.

Building these buffers is made easier with the CD3D11_BUFFER_DESC class provided with Windows 8. To build an immutable vertex buffer you just need the following code:

```
CD3D11_BUFFER_DESC desc = CD3D11_BUFFER_DESC(
sizeof(VertexPositionNormal) * NumVerts,
D3D11_BIND_VERTEX_BUFFER,
D3D11_USAGE_IMMUTABLE);
```

Setting the buffers

Now that we have a description that can be used to create the buffer as well as the vertex data, we can go about actually creating the buffer resource for use by the GPU. To do this we need our ID3D11Device1 pointer, and the CreateBuffer() method, used as follows:

```
PositionNormalVertex vertices[];
D3D11_BUFFER_DESC vertDesc;

// code to create the above items

ID3D11Buffer *pBuffer;
D3D11_SUBRESOURCE_DATA bufferData = {0};
bufferData.pSysMem = vertices;
bufferData.SysMemPitch = 0;
bufferData.SysMemSlicePitch = 0;
M_d3dDevice->CreateBuffer(&vertDesc, &bufferData, &pBuffer);
```

The preceding code creates an `ID3D11Buffer` object which contains our vertex buffer as described in our buffer description structure, and prefilled with data from our vertex array. Remember it's a similar method for the index buffer, but instead of our vertex array, you just need an array of integers.

The middle parameter is a `D3D11_SUBRESOURCE_DATA` object. You can use this object to point to the data in system memory that you want to load into the buffer by setting `pSysMem` to the pointer to your data. The other options just need to be set to zero for these buffers.

Using the buffers

You now know how to create the vertex and index buffers required for your model; however, there are a few more parts required before you will see anything on the screen. Before we get into the other requirements, let's run through how to actually use the buffers you have created.

In the graphics pipeline, before any of the shaders, we have the **input assembler**. This is responsible for handling and working with the vertex data that the shaders will operate on. We need to use the device context to set the vertex and index buffers on the input assembler, so that, when we have our **input layout** and **shaders** later on, it will have the data required to render.

The device context has a number of methods for interacting with the different parts of the pipeline, and each of them has a two-letter acronym at the start, which indicates the part of the pipeline the method operates on. In this case we want to look for methods beginning with IA, as follows:

- `IASetVertexBuffers`
- `IASetIndexBuffer`

We'll use these two methods to set the buffers on the GPU. Both are pretty straightforward, but for reference the following are the prototypes for each of them:

```
void IASetVertexBuffers(UINT startSlot, UINT numBuffers,
ID3D11Buffer * const *ppVertexBuffers, const UINT *pStrides,
const UINT *pOffsets);
```

Starting from the beginning, `startSlot` defines the input slot that the first buffer in your array will be assigned to. In most cases you won't need to specify anything other than zero, however, a non-zero value will allow you to bind multiple arrays at once.

numBuffers describes the number of vertex buffers within the pointer passed to ppVertexBuffers. You can pass in a chain of buffers if required, which will be bound to sequential slots based on the values in pOffsets.

ppVertexBuffers is a pointer to an array of vertex buffers. In many cases you won't need multiple vertex buffers to be bound at once, but if you do, put them all together and point to the start of the array.

pStrides defines the size of each element for each buffer. This means that you need to pass an array of values to pStrides, one for each of the buffers you are setting.

pOffsets is similar, but, it defines the offset for each buffer. In this case, we are defining the offset from the start of the buffer to the start of the vertices that need to be rendered for each buffer (as opposed to an offset from the start of ppVertexBuffers to the actual buffer).

For the index buffer, use the following method:

```
void IASetIndexBuffer(ID3D11Buffer *pIndexBuffer,
  DXGI_FORMAT format,
UINT offset);
```

For an index buffer you can only pass one buffer, so we just need the pointer to the buffer, as well as the format of each element and the offset to the start of the array that we will use.

For reference the format of the elements can be as follows:

- DXGI_FORMAT_R16_UINT
- DXGI_FORMAT_R32_UINT

Rxx refers to the length of the unsigned integer, where xx can be 16 bits or 32 bits depending on which integer you chose for your buffer.

Constant buffers

We have vertices and indices in place, and the matrices from the camera are ready, but how do we get those matrices up to the GPU? The answer is another buffer! This time we use a constant buffer to define constants for the shader stage that we will cover in the next section.

A constant buffer is a simple block of data that can be updated as required and transferred to the GPU. Creating the constant buffer is pretty much the same as the vertex or index buffer; however, you want to ensure you have CPU write access and the bind flag set to D3D11_BIND_CONSTANT_BUFFER. Using D3D11_USAGE_DYNAMIC for the usage flag is recommended here, as you will probably be updating this buffer each frame. You can avoid the sync cost by reusing the buffer as much as possible.

When setting up the shaders in the next stage, use the following commands to set a constant buffer on the vertex shader and pixel shader, respectively:

```
ID3D11Buffer *buffer;
// ... setup your constant buffer

m_d3dContext->VSSetConstantBuffers(0, 1, &buffer);
m_d3dContext->PSSetConstantBuffers(0, 1, &buffer);
```

Updating the buffers

Now that you know how to create and set the buffers, you need to know how to update them so they have the latest data. In many cases you won't need to do this; however, items such as constant buffers may require updating each frame.

First you need to ensure you've chosen the right usage type and CPU access flags during creation to ensure that you are allowed to update the buffer. Along with that it is important to remember that a usage type of DYNAMIC only allows for the use of the Map() method for updating.

Mapping the buffer

The first method for updating a buffer involves mapping the buffer to system memory and copying your data into that memory block. Direct3D will handle taking the data as it is copied and copying it to the graphics hardware. To do this, ID3D11DeviceContext provides a Map() command, as shown in the following code snippet:

```
m_d3dContext->Map(
resourceToMap,
subresource,
  mapType,
  mapFlags,
  pMappedResource
);
```

Here you need to specify the resource to map; this would be your `D3D11Buffer` pointer, and the index of the subresource, which in many cases will stay at zero.

After that you need to specify what type of mapping will occur. There are a few options to choose from depending on what you intend to do. They are as follows:

- `D3D11_MAP_READ`
- `D3D11_MAP_WRITE`
- `D3D11_MAP_READ_WRITE`
- `D3D11_MAP_WRITE_DISCARD`
- `D3D11_MAP_WRITE_NO_OVERWRITE`

`D3D11_MAP_WRITE_DISCARD` tells the GPU to discard the previous contents of the buffer upon mapping, meaning that you cannot read from the buffer, and if you don't write anything the GPU will read undefined memory. In this case the resource must be created with CPU write access and a `DYNAMIC` usage.

You will generally provide zero for the `mapFlags` parameter, which when set with the `D3D11_MAP_FLAG_DO_NOT_WAIT` will return an error and continue rather than waiting for the GPU to finish with the resource.

This method provides a `D3D11_MAPPED_SUBRESOURCE` object, which contains a pointer to the data you need to update, as well as some details about it. You can operate on the `pData` attribute depending on your access permissions.

Once you're done, just unmap the data using the following call:

```
m_d3dContext->Unmap(resource, subresource);
```

The UpdateSubresource() method

There is another method that lets you update data using a single function call; however, it does not work in all situations.

> For further details on when you can use the `UpdateSubresource()` method, please check the MSDN documentation for `ID3D11Device Context::UpdateSubresource()` at
>
> http://msdn.microsoft.com/en-us/library/windows/desktop/ff476486

```
M_d3dContext->UpdateSubresource(
   Resource,
   Subresource,
   destBox,
   sourceData,
   rowPitch,
   depthPitch
);
```

Here the `destBox` refers to the portion of data that should be changed with this operation. Rather than replacing everything you can update just a subsection of the resource, which can save time. If you pass `nullptr` to this, you will update the entire resource.

`rowPitch` refers to the size of one row of the source data. For many buffers you can just pass in the size of the row, however, if you were updating a texture you would pass in the size of the width in bytes, and then specify the `depthPitch` as the total size of the 2D texture.

With both the `UpdateSubresource()` and `Map()` methods, there are many gotchas and potential issues that you need to watch for. Be sure to read through the MSDN reference for both the options so you know which one you should use for your situation.

Shaders

We need two more things before we can actually render a 3D object. The first, and most important one, is the set of shaders that we will use to define the look of the object and tell the GPU what to do.

A shader is a small program written in a custom language (in this case, the High Level Shader Language—HLSL) that describes how the different stages of the pipeline will operate to render to the screen. There are a few different types of shaders; however, we only really need to cover the vertex and pixel shaders before any 3D rendering can be done.

Vertex shaders

The first shader that we will look at is the vertex shader. This shader is responsible for taking the vertices from our buffer and making sure they are in the right place relative to the virtual camera in the world.

A common vertex shader looks like the following:

```
cbuffer WVP : register(b0)
{
matrix World;
matrix View;
matrix Projection;
};

float3 main(float3 inputPos : POSITION) : POSITION
{
  float4 pos = float4(inputPos, 1.0f);
  pos = mul(pos, World);
  pos = mul(pos, View);
  pos = mul(pos, Projection);
  return pos;
}
```

HLSL has a C-like syntax that should make it easy to understand, so we'll focus on the new parts.

At the top you'll notice the `cbuffer` block. This is our shader representation of a constant buffer that we create in our game. In this case we provide three matrices, the world transform, the view transform, and the projection transform. We'll use these to take the vertex through to screen space, ready for the pixel shader.

Next you'll notice the definition of main, with some interesting additions to the parameters. The POSITION part is the semantic for the variable. This tells the GPU where to use this variable in the overall pipeline. With this you can link the inputPos variable to the position of the vertex. At the same time, we apply the POSITION semantic to the function to tell the GPU that we want to use the float3 return value as the output POSITION.

Pixel shaders

Pixel shaders represent the final step in the rendering pipeline that you can control. Once a vertex emerges from the vertex shader, the pipeline determines which pixels make up the surface of the triangle, and uses the pixel shader to draw each one, interpolating between the vertices as required to provide input to the pixel shader.

A very simple pixel shader that sets the entire model to a single color has the following code:

```
float4 main(float4 pos : POSITION) : SV_TARGET
{
   return float4(1.0f, 0, 0, 1.0f);
}
```

This is quite short; however, it illustrates what you need to provide to successfully render something. In particular, you need to set the SV_TARGET semantic to tell the pipeline what color to put at that position. To do this, we need to return a float4 that describes the color using the red, green, blue, and alpha channels, in that order. Setting a value of 1.0f on a channel indicates we want 100 percent of that color in the final mixed RGB value, and in this case we will see red in the shape of the model.

Pixel shaders really become powerful when they are used to add lighting and shading to objects. These effects can range from simple calculations (N dot L lighting calculation), to advanced global illumination (light bounces around the scene to realistically provide ambient lighting).

Compiling and loading

We now need to load these shaders into our program, compile them, and load them onto the GPU. One important thing to note here is that you cannot compile shaders once they have been submitted to the Windows Store, so you need to make sure you precompile the shaders and load them in (from the file or from within the code) as byte-code shaders when you want to submit to the store. During development you are allowed to use the compiler within your application if you want; however, once you are ready to submit you need to precompile the shaders.

There are a few ways to load in your code, and the Direct3D sample provides a helper method that reads all the data from a file. Once you have the data, though, you need to use the Direct3D device to create the shader.

 If you give your shader the .hlsl file extension and add it to your project, Visual Studio 2012 will compile it for you and output an object file that you can load directly without worrying about a custom compile step.

To load in the shader you need to call the appropriate CreateXXShader method, where XX is the type of shader. To create the vertex shader, you can use the following method:

```
ID3D11VertexShader *shader;
m_d3dDevice->CreateVertexShader(
file->Data,
file->Length,
nullptr,
  &shader
);
```

The first two parameters are standard: the unsigned char array that contains the bytes for the shader data and the length of the data. The third parameter provides the class linkage data. However, unless you're working with the advanced features in **Shader Model 5** you won't need this; passing the nullptr is fine. Finally you get the shader from the final parameter using a pointer to an ID3D11VertexShaderpointer. Pixel shaders are similar; just change the name.

Input layouts

Now we have shaders and the different buffers that we need to render. There's just one more crucial component before we can draw anything. We give our vertices to the API, and in the shader we request input data based on semantics, but how does the API know which parts of each vertex to match to each semantic?

This is done through an input layout, which is just a description of the layout of your vertex element, along with annotations to indicate which part matches which semantic. Just like most items in Direct3D11, you need to fill out a description structure before you can create the input layout with the device. A typical layout may look like the following code snippet:

```
const D3D11_INPUT_ELEMENT_DESC vertexDesc[] =
{
{ "POSITION", 0, DXGI_FORMAT_R32G32B32_FLOAT, 0, 0,
D3D11_INPUT_PER_VERTEX_DATA, 0 },
  { "COLOR",    0, DXGI_FORMAT_R32G32B32_FLOAT, 0, 12,
D3D11_INPUT_PER_VERTEX_DATA, 0 },
};
```

Each of the `D3D11_INPUT_ELEMENT_DESC` structures consists of the following pieces of data:

```
typedef struct D3D11_INPUT_ELEMENT_DESC
    {
    LPCSTR SemanticName;
    UINT SemanticIndex;
    DXGI_FORMAT Format;
    UINT InputSlot;
    UINT AlignedByteOffset;
    D3D11_INPUT_CLASSIFICATION InputSlotClass;
    UINT InstanceDataStepRate;
    }   D3D11_INPUT_ELEMENT_DESC;
```

It begins with the semantic name, of which there are many different options. At the very least you require a `POSITION` attribute and everything else is optional. The most commonly used semantics are as follows:

- `POSITION`
- `COLOR`
- `NORMAL`
- `TEXCOORD`

`TEXCOORD` refers to the texture coordinate on the model, which is a `float2`/`vector2` attribute describing the **UV coordinates** at that vertex.

 UV coordinates refer to the part of the texture displayed at that point, and exist as a value between zero and one.

Semantics do not require that they only exist once within a vertex structure. Some, like the texture coordinate, can have multiple versions, referred to in HLSL using a number at the end of the semantic (`TEXCOORD0`, `TEXCOORD1`, and so on).

The second parameter in this structure lets you define which one this particular attribute refers to. In most cases this can just remain at zero; however, if you need multiple normal or texture coordinates, this would be the place to specify which index it has.

The format defines the data type stored in that attribute. You need to ensure you match the data type, and number of channels or parts to what it actually stores to ensure it is read properly. Some commonly used formats are the following:

- `DXGI_FORMAT_R32G32B32_FLOAT`
- `DXGI_FORMAT_R32G32_FLOAT`
- `DXGI_FORMAT_R32_FLOAT`

There are also variations of these for signed and unsigned integers (SINT and UINT, respectively).

After that you need to define which Input Slot this attribute exists in. You can get away with setting this to zero in most cases. If you are working with multiple vertex buffers, you would use this parameter to specify which buffer this attribute applies to.

`AlignedByteOffset` refers to the offset from the start of the element to the start of the attribute. If you are defining these attributes sequentially you can use the helper `D3D11_APPEND_ALIGNED_ELEMENT`, which will automatically determine the correct offset based on the earlier description.

`InputSlotClass` refers to the `D3D11_INPUT_CLASSIFICATION` descriptor for the attribute. Unless you are working with instancing, this will always be `D3D11_INPUT_PER_VERTEX_DATA`.

Finally `InstanceDataStepRate` can just be set to zero if you aren't working with instancing. This value specifies the number of instances that should be drawn before advancing to the next element in the instance data buffer.

With all of this information we just need a quick call to the `CreateInputLayout()` method on the device and we will have an input layout ready for use. The following is what that call looks like:

```
M_d3dDevice->CreateInputLayout(
    vertexDesc,
    2, // Size of the vertex description array
    vsFile->Data,
    vsFile->Length,
    &m_inputLayout
);
```

Here we started by passing the array of vertex descriptors, and telling the device how many descriptors exist within the array. Then we need to pass in the vertex shader file that this input layout will be mapped to. We need to do this because vertex shaders may expect different layouts and we need to ensure that everything matches up; otherwise, there will be a miscommunication and error.

Finally we receive an `ID3D11InputLayout*` object that we can use when drawing to specify the layout to be used with the set shader.

Drawing the model

Once everything has been created and loaded, we can look at drawing the vertices to the screen using the specified shader. There are a couple of steps before which we can call the `Draw()` method; however, these are all simple method calls to indicate we will use each resource.

A quick note on topology

Topology defines how Direct3D will read and interpret the provided indices or vertices to lay out the mesh. When drawing the mesh, it can be optimized to reduce the number of required vertices and indices by reusing the last two indices when drawing. This is referred to as a **triangle strip**. Consuming and using the vertices and indices as originally described would involve a triangle list, which is the simplest and often most compatible topology that can be used for drawing triangles, as a strip requires extra processing to ensure the order is correct without breaking the model.

Other options such as lines and points also exist, and these notify Direct3D that you don't want shaded triangles to be drawn. Instead, the vertices should be drawn as points, or lines between vertices, allowing for different techniques to be used. This would be a good option if you were looking to draw a wireframe, as you can construct the data using two vertices (or indices) for each line and draw them without having to worry about how to draw lines using rectangles and triangles.

This is a list of commonly used primitive topologies, as defined in the `D3D_PRIMITIVE_TOPOLOGY` enumeration:

- `D3D11_PRIMITIVE_TOPOLOGY_POINTLIST`
- `D3D11_PRIMITIVE_TOPOLOGY_LINELIST`
- `D3D11_PRIMITIVE_TOPOLOGY_TRIANGLELIST`
- `D3D11_PRIMITIVE_TOPOLOGY_TRIANGLESTRIP`

Setting the buffers and drawing

You generally want to follow the given order for drawing a model:

1. Set the vertex buffer.
2. Set the index buffer.

3. Set the primitive topology.

4. Set the input layout.

5. Set the vertex shader.

6. Set the pixel shader.

7. Set the constant buffer(s).

8. Draw the model.

We've covered how to set buffers, so ensure that they're set at the appropriate times during the drawing phase. Instead we'll focus on setting the rest of the content.

To set the primitive topology, we need to call the following method:

```
m_d3dContext->IASetPrimitiveTopology(
D3D11_PRIMITIVE_TOPOLOGY_TRIANGLELIST
);
```

You'll note that again all of these methods define the pipeline stage using two letters at the start of the method. In this case we're still working with the input assembler; however, after this you'll notice that we have moved onto the vertex shader and pixel shader.

Now we need to set the layout using the simple `IASetInputLayout()` method, which just takes a pointer to the input layout as a parameter.

After this, the shaders need to be set. To set the vertex shader, you have to call the following line:

```
m_d3dContext->VSSetShader(
  vertexShader,
  nullptr,
  0
);
```

Here the only parameter that you need to worry about is the first one, which specifies the `D3D11VertexShader` object. The other two lines refer to Shader Model 5 classes, which is far outside the scope of this appendix.

To set a pixel shader you can use pretty much the same method, with the only difference being that you call the `PSSetShader()` method instead of the `VSSetShader()`.

Now we just need to set the constant buffer on the vertex shader so that it has the camera data required to perform the transform. To do this, you have to make the following call:

```
m_d3dContext->VSSetConstantBuffers(
    0,
    1,
    &pConstantBuffer
);
```

Here you will specify the slot the constant buffer will be placed in, and the number of buffers within the array. Like the `IASetVertexBuffers`, you can set multiple buffers at once. Finally, you need to point to the array of buffer pointers. In this case we only have one element in the array so we just pass the pointer to the `pConstantBuffer`.

Finally we have everything in place, and we can execute the command to draw this model to the screen. There are a couple of different draw calls depending on whether you're using an index buffer, or performing instancing. If you want to draw without an index buffer, it's a simple call to the following:

```
m_d3dContext->Draw(
    vertCount,
    startingVertex
);
```

This is pretty simple; you have to specify the total number of vertices, and the index of the first vertex to start drawing from, usually zero.

If you are using an index buffer, you can use the following method:

```
m_d3dContext->DrawIndexed(
    indexCount,
    startingIndex,
    baseVertex
);
```

This is pretty similar to the last one; however, here you can also define which vertex in your buffer represents index 0. Sometimes, you may want to use this when you have multiple meshes within a single vertex buffer and you have index buffers for each mesh rather than the entire buffer. You can rebase the vertex buffer so that you're referring to the correct vertices.

Summary

You've done it; you now have enough knowledge to start creating games in 3D with Direct3D11. In this appendix, we went through the different objects that you need, from vertices and indices to buffers and input layouts. We looked at how to create all of these, update them, and use them to draw a collection of vertices. Hopefully, you can take the information in this section as a reference to assist in developing your 3D development skills further. Many of the enumerations and parameters you can use have been listed for reference, so keep this appendix handy, or build up a list of MSDN articles that can give you the information you need to choose the right option.

Index

E

EndGame() 125
EndGame method 126, 138
Export Control Classification Number (ECCN) 169
Extensible Application Markup Language. *See* XAML
Extensions and Updates dialog 32

F

farZ parameter 201
field of view (fov) 201
file formats
  DXT 35
  PNG 34
FindAllPeersAsync() method 155
font
  building 44, 45
  drawing 46
FontSize parameter 45
FontStyle parameter 45
Frame 12, 13
frame delta 25
Frames Per Second (FPS) 12
freemium model 183, 184
front buffer 15
FrontToBack option 41
frustum 201

G

game
  components 65
  entity 65, 66, 67
  Load method 70
  orientation 112
  Player->BindInput method 72
  pool of enemies, creating 74
  progression 124, 125
  selling 181-183
  Ship class 69
  state 124, 125, 126
  structuring 64
  submitting 167, 168, 176
  subsystems 75, 76
  texture, origin 70

traditional object-oriented approach 64, 65
  Update method 74
  uploading 175, 176
Game::Update method 99
Game::Update() method 53
GameApplication class 51, 53
GameApplication.cpp file 55
Game Definition File. *See* GDF
Game->Load() function 46
game lobby 153
game loop
  about 24
  back buffer, presenting 27, 28
  screen, clearing 26, 27
  simulation, updating 24
  world, drawing 25
GamePad
  about 50, 56-58
  buttons 59, 60
  Deadzones and thumbsticks 60, 61
  multiple controllers 59
GDF
  about 168
  certificates 168, 169
Geocoordinate Position property 119
Geocoordinate type 119
Geographic North 111
geolocator->GetGeopositionAsync() method 120
geometry shader 23
GetBuffer() method 20
GetCurrentReading() method 109, 116
GetDefault() method 109, 112, 117
GetGeopositionAsync() method 120
get() method 187
GetTemplateContent 137
GPS
  about 105, 117
  polling 120
  position 119
  status 118, 119
GPU 34
graphics pipeline 23, 24
Graphics Processing Unit. *See* GPU
gyro->GetCurrentReading() method 110
Gyrometer class 109
gyroscope 105, 109

X

Y

About Packt Publishing

Packt, pronounced 'packed', published its first book "*Mastering phpMyAdmin for Effective MySQL Management*" in April 2004 and subsequently continued to specialize in publishing highly focused books on specific technologies and solutions.

Our books and publications share the experiences of your fellow IT professionals in adapting and customizing today's systems, applications, and frameworks. Our solution based books give you the knowledge and power to customize the software and technologies you're using to get the job done. Packt books are more specific and less general than the IT books you have seen in the past. Our unique business model allows us to bring you more focused information, giving you more of what you need to know, and less of what you don't.

Packt is a modern, yet unique publishing company, which focuses on producing quality, cutting-edge books for communities of developers, administrators, and newbies alike. For more information, please visit our website: www.packtpub.com.

Writing for Packt

We welcome all inquiries from people who are interested in authoring. Book proposals should be sent to author@packtpub.com. If your book idea is still at an early stage and you would like to discuss it first before writing a formal book proposal, contact us; one of our commissioning editors will get in touch with you.

We're not just looking for published authors; if you have strong technical skills but no writing experience, our experienced editors can help you develop a writing career, or simply get some additional reward for your expertise.

jQuery Game Development Essentials

ISBN: 978-1-84969-506-0   Paperback: 244 pages

Learn how to make fun and addictive multi-platform games using jQuery

1. Discover how you can create a fantastic RPG, arcade game, or platformer using jQuery!

2. Learn how you can integrate your game with various social networks, creating multiplayer experiences and also ensuring compatibility with mobile devices.

3. Create your very own framework, harnessing the very best design patterns and proven techniques along the way.

Windows Phone 8 Game Development

ISBN: 978-1-84969-680-7   Paperback: 394 pages

A practical guide to creating games for the Windows Phone 8 platform

1. Create a 3D game for the Windows Phone 8 platform

2. Combine native and managed development approaches

3. Discover how to use a range of inputs, including sensors

4. Learn how to implement geolocation and augmented reality features

Please check **www.PacktPub.com** for information on our titles

Yii Application Development Cookbook - Second Edition

ISBN: 978-1-78216-310-7   Paperback: 408 pages

A Cookbook covering both practical Yii application development tips and the most important Yii features

1. Learn how to use Yii even more efficiently

2. Full of practically useful solutions and concepts you can use in your application

3. Both important Yii concept descriptions and practical recipes are inside

Learning Libgdx Game Development

ISBN: 978-1-78216-604-7   Paperback: 388 pages

Walk through a complete game development cycle with practical examples and build cross-platform games with Libgdx

1. Create a libGDX multi-platform game from start to finish

2. Learn about the key features of libGDX that will ease and speed up your development cycles

3. Write your game code once and run it on a multitude of platforms using libGDX

Please check **www.PacktPub.com** for information on our titles

www.ingramcontent.com/pod-product-compliance
Lightning Source LLC
LaVergne TN
LVHW062313060326
832902LV00013B/2190